Praise for
This Is Me* and *Watch This

"*This Is Me* will encourage, inspire, and challenge anyone who dives in. Many girls and women feel too scared or uncomfortable to talk about these issues with a guy. For that reason, this book poses a uniqueness that separates it from the pack. Not only is Jeffrey's approach on a very personal level, it's packed with biblical truths. This book will change your life if you're a young lady, a mother, or even a guy!"

—JOSH REEDY, lead singer, DecembeRadio

"In *Watch This*, Jeffrey uses biblical truth to encourage teen guys to grow toward authentic manhood."

—JASON ROY, lead singer, Building 429

"Jeffrey Dean has a way of zeroing in on today's youth culture. He knows teens and how to communicate the love of Jesus to them in a way that captures their attention and convicts their hearts."

—JOSH D. MCDOWELL, author and communicator

"Jeffrey Dean's *This Is Me* reads like an honest conversation with a trusted big brother. No catchy gimmicks or watered down lessons—just straight talk about the things girls care about most, backed up by Scripture, with all the authenticity that today's teens long for. I can't wait to share it with the girls in my life!"

—SHELLEY BREEN, singer, Point of Grace, and coauthor of *Life, Love, and Other Mysteries*

"In both *This Is Me* and *Watch This*, Jeffrey Dean has done a great job of identifying the things that matter most in life and conveying a message of hope for teens. His words are timeless and strong. You'll love what you read, because it connects with the very heart of God."

—DANIEL S. WOLGEMUTH, President/CEO, Youth for Christ

"*This Is Me* is one of the most thorough, honest, biblical, and compassionate books I have read in quite some time. It's the kind of message I believe God will use to touch many teenagers across America. Jeffrey Dean is not only a talented musician and communicator, but God has given him a deep love for today's teenagers, and it shows. I highly recommend his work to you."

—DAWSON MCALLISTER, national talk show host

"Among student communicators I've heard, I rate Jeffrey Dean among the top five. His message is relevant, clear, and biblical. He has a unique ability to relate to students about their culture and the choices they face. I highly recommend him."

—PHIL WALDREP, Phil Waldrep Ministries, Trinity, Alabama

"Jeffrey is a gifted and passionate speaker who connects with teens at all levels. He is insightful and relevant—speaking into today's issues with the boldness that contemporary student culture requires."

—RON KECK, managing director, Serendipity House Publishing

"I am always amazed at the energy and enthusiasm that Jeffrey Dean brings to his work with teens. And his enthusiasm is contagious! Jeffrey's abstinence message has been an extremely valuable resource for our clubs—becoming, in fact, the perfect vehicle to carry this all-important message to our young people. I know first-hand that Jeffrey's message is not only getting into our schools and youth facilities, but it's being listened to and taken to heart by kids."

—JOHN HOLLIS, director of development, Boys and Girls Clubs of Delaware

"Jeffrey's stories are true, his facts are accurate, and his message to teens about making today's choices count for the future is heard loud and clear."

—LESLEE J. UNRUH, president of the Abstinence Clearinghouse

this is me

this is me

a teen girl's guide to becoming the real you

jeffrey dean

MULTNOMAH
BOOKS

THIS IS ME
PUBLISHED BY MULTNOMAH BOOKS
12265 Oracle Boulevard, Suite 200
Colorado Springs, Colorado 80921
A division of Random House Inc.

ISBN: 978-1-59052-985-0

Library of Congress Cataloging-in-Publication Data
Dean, Jeffrey.
This is me : a teen girl's guide to becoming the real you / by Jeffrey Dean. — 1st ed.
p. cm.
ISBN 978-1-59052-985-0
1. Teenage girls—Religious life. 2. Teenage girls—Conduct of life. I. Title.
BV4551.3.D43 2007
248.8'33—dc22

2007010434

Printed in the United States of America
2007—First Edition

10 9 8 7 6 5 4 3 2 1

To Bailey and Brynn

Contents

Acknowledgments

Many thanks to Adrienne Spain. It was even better this time around. Your talent inspires me. Thank you again. To David Kopp and everyone at Multnomah. Thank you to the many Prayer Partners of *Jeffrey Dean Ministries.* To all of my family. To my girls—you are my joy. To Amy—I love you. To teen girls everywhere—as you read this book, I pray you see yourself as God sees you. To God be the glory.

Chapter 1

Who You Are, Really

When being the "It" girl just isn't enough.

Heather was an extremely shy and soft-spoken freshman. One of her teachers introduced her to me when I spoke at her school. It only took a few minutes for me to see Heather was lonely and very insecure. As we were talking, several girls walked by and made a crude comment about her. My heart broke for her. She told me she didn't have many friends. She even asked me what I thought she should do to make more friends. I was hurting for Heather, but as I watched her walk back to class, I knew there was no way I could understand how hard life really was for her…

Renee was a popular, smart, funny senior in high school, and she had a singing voice that made Britney Spears sound like Miss Piggy. (Actually Britney Spears does that all on her own.) Renee and her boyfriend, Reed, stopped me backstage at a conference where I spoke. They were both in the band that led worship that night. Renee was a preacher's kid. Ask her a question about the Bible, and she had all the right answers. "When your daddy is the one in the pulpit, you kind of have to act like you've got it all together," she said. But I could tell Renee was far from having it "all together."

The more we talked, the more the facade began to fade. She said, "I can't remember the last time I had a real conversation with my dad. He's so busy doing church that he hardly ever has time for me." And then, as I continued to listen, she confirmed what I had already suspected: "Reed and I are sleeping together. I know it's wrong. But we are." Obviously, her lack of attention from her father left a void in her heart she was trying to fill with a cute guy and sexual intimacy. It *was* wrong. And I could tell that, deep down, she knew it…

Sarah was sixteen when I met her at a camp in Texas. She introduced herself by saying, "Hi, I'm Sarah, and I'm dying." Talk about an introduction. It was one of those awkward slo-mo moments where you really don't know what to say. Wanting to keep the conversation positive, I responded and said something *really* smart: "Hi, Sarah. I'm Jeffrey, and I don't like cheese." Yes, it sounds as stupid now as it did then. I'm still learning that if you don't have anything smart to say, sometimes you should just say nothing.

Sarah told me about the day she heard the news that she had leukemia. She talked about chemo, pain, losing her hair, and a fear of dying. She was mad at God, mad at the world, and basically mad at everything and everyone. (Who wouldn't be, right?) "I haven't lived a perfect life or anything," she said. "But I don't deserve this. It's just not fair!" Sarah's reality was difficult for her to understand. It was difficult for me to understand. I might have told her that a lot of things in life seem unfair and they aren't always easy to explain, but that wouldn't be what she wanted—or needed—to hear. So, rather than once again saying something I might regret, I just listened as she talked. That's what she really needed…

Then there's Lisa. She's a cheerleader. She told me how difficult it was to live the life of a Christian while also being a cheerleader on her high-school campus. She talked about post-high-school plans of college and eventually Bible school. She wanted to be a missionary.

"My friends respect me, but they also think I'm a little crazy to believe in all this Jesus stuff," she said. "I want to honor God with my life, but it isn't always easy, and honestly, it isn't always fun." She shared with me that lately things had been tough—her parents divorced at the end of her junior year. I could tell Lisa really wanted to live right. But I could also tell she was struggling with trying to figure out if living right was really worth it for her…

Heather, Renee, Sarah, Lisa: Their stories are different, but they share a common theme. All these girls want more—more than what they have right now. They can't see themselves as they really are or what they can be, because they haven't realized God has a very special purpose for each girl—a purpose he created them to fulfill. Believe it or not, he created every single one of us with a unique plan in mind. When these girls realize this purpose exists, they'll find out who God made them to be. The same goes for you.

A Little Confession

In case you didn't notice yet, I'm not a girl. I'm not even a teen. But I've spent over a decade in youth ministry listening to teen girls share their stories, and it was their pain, their confusion, and their hope that made me believe I could write this book. Still, why wouldn't I just leave girls' books to women writers? They know more about your life and understand you better, right? Well, that may be true, but I can offer you something they can't—a guy's perspective. I thought you might be interested to know what goes on in guys' heads. If you are, I can help you with that.

Of course, I'm not only writing this book to give you advice on boys. I may know a few things, but definitely not enough for a whole book. What I want to talk to you about most is God's truth. We live in a world of untruths. Lots of girls like you don't have many adults in their lives willing to stand in front of them and tell them the truth. It's hard to get a straight answer—whether it's about guys, sex, God, or yourself. Lots of adults today are more concerned with getting you to like them than with telling you what you need to hear. And lots of people want to convince you there are no absolute truths, that everything, even the most basic biblical lessons, can be questioned. You can start to feel like it doesn't matter what you do because there's really no right or wrong. I want to show you there *are* choices that are absolutely right and choices that are absolutely wrong. I want to be the guy who'll be straight with you about the things that matter most, because these are the things that'll help you feel better about yourself and your place in the world.

More to Life

Take a minute to look deep into your heart and ask yourself these questions:

- Do I want more from life than what I have right now?
- Am I unfulfilled?
- Are there some past choices I've made that I regret?
- Do I feel like something is missing from my life?
- Is there an emptiness inside me that I try to fill with worldly solutions that don't work?
- Can I be a better woman than I am right now?

If you answered yes to any of those questions, you're who I wrote this book for. *This Is Me* is a guide to becoming the woman God made you to be. This means finding fulfillment, filling your emptiness, and having more than you ever imagined possible. You live in a world that a lot of times doesn't value who you *really* are but who you can *pretend* to be. The makeup, the clothes, the hair, the performance to win over the boys—it's easy to lose the real you. I want to help you discover the person God made you to be and the purpose he created you to fulfill. When you seek and eventually discover this purpose, you'll stop feeling like you're always falling short and finally start feeling complete—and content with who you are.

take a break

How's your life? Take a minute and write how you feel about your life right now. I feel confused. Sometimes I feel alone, like I'm on a battlefeild and I'm the only one up against in army.

What frustrates you the most about your life?
That it seems I get stuck with hard decisions and I am sometimes alone.

What about your life makes you smile?
That I have people that back me up and see thing in me that I can't even see myself.

Who Are You?

Recently a sixteen-year-old girl named Jennifer approached me after I spoke at her school. She said, "I feel like I'm always trying to be what everyone else wants me to be instead of just being who I want to be." When I asked her why, she simply said, "I just want to be liked." She told me she'd changed the color of her hair, had dieted, and had even slept with several guys, all in an attempt to feel accepted. Jennifer was desperate for attention. She was desperate for acceptance. And she was willing to become whoever and whatever she thought was necessary in order to fit in.

I totally understand how Jennifer felt. Don't you? One of the greatest pressures you face is the pressure to fit in, to find acceptance. I call this the "It" dilemma. You want to be It. You want to do It. No matter what It is at the moment, you have to do It, be It, have It. And the It is always changing. So the pressure is unrelenting. And happiness never lasts.

What *He's* Thinking

You think guys never feel insecure or pressured to fit in? You might be surprised to know that guys are not immune to any of that. They may hide it better, but they're struggling just like you are. Is the guy you like sweet to you when you're alone, but then he ignores you when his buddies are around? He could just be a jerk—but probably he doesn't want his friends to think he's weak or "whipped." Just remember, boys feel the pressure too, so you can find a little comfort in the fact that girls aren't the only ones.

Lots of girls I've counseled have told me about struggling with this It problem. They may not realize it, but when they're trying to achieve It status, they're really searching for popularity, acceptance, love, security, or self-worth, just like Jennifer. But that search is leading many of them on an endless quest for It rather than becoming the woman God created them to be.

You may think that becoming, having, or doing It will make you feel complete. But I think you're smart enough to know somewhere deep down that it won't. It might feel really good for a while, but it won't last. The definition of It is always changing, so your goal is always moving just out of your reach, forcing you to become something new again and again. Trying to live up to the world's expectations can lead you straight into trouble...and pain. Because, by the world's standards:

- you'll never be good enough
- you'll never be beautiful enough
- you'll never be skinny enough
- you'll never be sexy enough
- you'll never be smart enough

Unless you get focused on the only It that matters—God's purpose for you—you'll get confused by all kinds of other things, things that seem important but eventually fade away. Satan wants nothing more than to confuse you and convince you that you can never be the woman God made you to be. Yes, God made you for a very specific purpose—and he made you for more than what the others at school think is cool. Satan is working overtime to convince you that fulfillment isn't found in pursuing God's plan for your life but only in striving to be It. But really, the more you try to achieve It, the more you'll feel like you'll *never* be enough.

So if your life isn't just about family and friends and parties and boys and popularity and living day to day without a guide or a goal, then what is it about? The answer is pretty simple—and pretty complicated. It's about *something more.*

At your age, you're going through all the cliché teenager stuff that means you're "growing up"—your body is changing, you're learning to drive, and adults are always exclaiming about how much you've grown and asking if you have a boyfriend. But becoming a woman is not just about growing older. (I'm sure you can think of a few people who are older than you who don't act like "adults" at all.) You don't choose whether or not you get older—you just do. But becoming a woman is a choice.

This "something more" I'm talking about is different for everyone. Right now you may be thinking, *If you can't tell me what it is, then how am I supposed to find it?* Well, it isn't about figuring it all out right now. It *is* about trust. God does have a plan for you, and he's not going to hide it from you. He wants you to know what it is. You just have to trust him. Are you willing to trust God that much?

> Trust in the LORD with all your heart
> and lean not on your own understanding;
> in all your ways acknowledge him,
> and he will make your paths straight.
> (Proverbs 3:5–6)

In other words, God is saying:

Give me a chance. Let me prove to you that I have it all under control.

Let me show you that I am capable of doing something amazing with your life.

Let me make you into the woman I created you to be.

Let me make you into the woman who will stand for me.

Let me use you to show the world who I am.

Maybe things in your life are okay right now. Nothing catastrophic has happened lately. But every time you look in the mirror, you find something wrong with yourself, something that's just got to be changed. Or maybe *everything* is wrong right now, and all you think about is how you have to change every single thing about yourself. If you want to have the ability to fight that feeling and look in the mirror and be happy (or at least happier) with what you see, you need to give God a chance. Things may be good, but he can make them great. Whether you're completely depressed or pretty happy, you always need God—because, in him, you can be so much more than you ever imagined you could be. You can be who he created you to be.

What You Need to Know as You Read

God's purpose may be different for every person, but there are some rules and advice that apply to everyone as they look for their purpose and then try to achieve it. First, I'll try to help you see how God feels about you. If you can see yourself the way God sees you, it'll make your life a lot easier—and happier. I'm also going to have chapters about all the usual teenager topics—sex, dating, family, and friends—so I can help you see how what you do in these areas can get you closer to God (and the closer you are to him, the easier it is to hear what he has to tell you). I'm also going to have chapters on evangelism, finding your purpose, and one about some of those problems that you usually keep secret. In all of these chapters, I'll share everything I know about God's truths and try to help you figure out how to live them out every day.

But before you start, there are five Foundational Truths you need to know as you read this book. It's critical that you understand these truths before you move on to the following chapters, because they'll help you get the most out of what you're about to read.

1. Don't just take my word for it.

When I was younger and I read books with a lot of scripture in them, most of the time I'd skip the scripture, just to save some time. If you do that with this book, you'll miss the good stuff. Each verse has been chosen for a very specific reason. So as you read, don't just take my word on a particular issue. Read the included scriptures. Contemplate. Go deeper. Ask questions. Don't just be challenged by me—be challenged by God in his Word.

2. If he says it, he means it.

Since I just established in Truth #1 that I'll share a ton of scriptures with you throughout this book, you need to know this: if God says it, he means it. There are some who teach that God's Word is no longer relevant to your life or that you don't have to do everything the Bible says. Don't buy it. The Bible is truth. It's from God. And it's God's gift to you to guide you on your journey. The point is—you can take God at his Word.

3. You've gotta be tough.

Following God is the best road, but it's not always the easiest. You don't have to apply the advice I give you in the following pages, but you'll have a really tough time becoming the woman God wants you to be if you don't. This book is not a walk-in-the-park, feel-good read.

Becoming a woman of God shouldn't be taken lightly. As you read, you'll need discipline, consistency, determination, and trust. And if you choose to apply these truths to your life, it's a choice that'll help transform you into his likeness and shape you into the person you were made to be. It'll be tough. But it'll be more than worth it.

4. Give me a chance.

There are probably a lot of books you can read written for girls by a girl. Obviously, this is not one of them. That's why this book is unique. Most likely there are few, if any, men in your life who'll talk to you as openly and honestly as I will in this book. Think of our time together as an intimate talk...with a guy. (How often does that happen?) I'll also pause sometimes to let you in on how guys feel about the things we're talking about together. You'll be surprised and, I hope, encouraged when you read some of my explanations.

However, while I'll be really good at giving you a guy's perspective on things and at sharing with you my knowledge of the Bible and what I've learned from counseling, I won't be as good at talking about some of the really girl-specific stuff that only girls can really understand. That's why, throughout the book, you'll see a voice, a girl's voice, coming in and calling me out on some of the stuff I'm missing or getting wrong. That voice, brought to you courtesy of a real (and very...how should I say it?...*inquisitive*) female, will keep me in check and hopefully ask some of the same things you're thinking as you read.

5. You can do this.

I'm going to be honest with you and really challenge you in these next chapters. I'll ask things of you that are more difficult than anything you've done before. But don't worry—though you can't become the woman God wants you to be by just cramming for the test the night before, the extra work will be worth it. There may be times as you're reading when you'll feel like throwing in the towel. But don't do it. Your walk with God isn't like getting spiritual plastic surgery. Everything's not fixed in an instant. It's a one-day-at-a-time thing. So don't give up. You can do this.

Why You Need to Keep Reading

First, this book will encourage you and remind you that you're worthy of God's love and meant to live out his purpose. As you start to see yourself as God sees you, you'll feel stronger, more confident, and more able to face the unavoidable challenges life in an imperfect world brings.

Also, this book can be a resource for you, a place to turn for help and advice. You'll sometimes face problems that seem insurmountable. And that's usually when Satan works overtime to mess up God's plan for your life. If you feel shaken, like you don't know what the right thing is (or the wrong thing just seems too good to pass up), this book will help you get refocused on what's really important.

Lastly, you probably have a lot of questions you're too embarrassed to ask anyone else, or maybe you don't know who to ask. I hope this book will be a place you can come to for answers. Inside all these chapters, I'll try to use my experience working with teenagers to answer some of your toughest questions. I won't pretend that I know everything—because I definitely don't—but I'll share what I've learned in my own walk with God and in helping other people with theirs.

You don't need to be perfect for God to work in you. You don't need someone to wave a magic wand and change you into someone new. You don't need to lie or pretend to be someone you're not. You just need to be willing to let God lead you, so you can be who he made you to be. Then you'll finally be able to say, "This is me. And I wouldn't change a thing."

Chapter 2

Being You and Liking It

Every girl gets confused...until she loses the lies.

You are beautiful."

"I accept you for who you are."

"I'll never walk away from you."

"You can always count on me."

"I'll never hurt you."

"I'll be here in the morning."

That's what everyone wants to hear, right? The older we get, the more we need the assurance of security, acceptance, love, and commitment. All those things that probably came really easily when we were young get harder and harder to find. Never having to let go. Never worrying about tomorrow. Never living in fear of abandonment, pain, and rejection. In countless counseling sessions with girls like you, again and again I seem to find one overwhelming need driving their hopes, dreams, struggles, and fears: They want to feel complete—no doubts, no questions. They want to hear those reassuring words—and believe them.

But instead, all you hear every day is that you need to change, that you're not good enough yet: "Look Like a Movie Star!" "Get the Body You Dream of in Thirty Days!" "Don't Get Played! You Do the Playing with the Right Body!" "Have the Sexiest Body on the Beach This Summer!" "Girl Falls in Love with Food—Dumps Boyfriend!" Okay, that last one has nothing to do with this chapter. I just thought it was funny.

Exclamations like that are plastered across the perfect faces of magazine cover models every month. And if you put down the magazine and turn on the television, things don't get any better. I've been watching MTV lately (for research purposes only—definitely not because I'm addicted to *My Super Sweet Sixteen*). Have you? If so, you may have noticed that things seem to get more and more outrageous.

MTV's a good example of what you see everywhere these days. From *Parental Control* to *Laguna Beach,* you meet girls with a lot of cleavage and very little clothing—and usually minimal brains and almost nonexistent morality. With their pretty blond hair and tiny waists, they hypnotize us, and we start believing we want to be like them. I mean, who wouldn't want to be the hottest girl in the Hollywood Hills or the cutest guy in the OC?

Write down five characteristics that best describe how women are portrayed in today's culture.

1. Skinny

2. Beautiful

3. Perfect

4. Superficial

5. Slutty

What kinds of words did you write? Were they positive, like *independent, sexy,* or *beautiful*? Or were they not so positive, like *slutty, superficial,* or *dumb*? Maybe you have some words from both categories.

On TV or in movies or magazines, women are often portrayed as:

1. People who are obsessed with their appearance
2. People who determine their value by how skinny and sexy they can be
3. People who are ready and willing to hook up whenever and wherever (because that's what guys want, right?)

It's as if "woman" has been stripped of almost every good, pure, and honorable quality. Instead, you're told that completion is found in beauty, sex, and money. And as you're probably already aware, those aren't exactly the best values to have.

The result of all this is that many girls have associated value and significance with weight and appearance; self-esteem with sex appeal; acceptance with becoming It. They've bought the cultural lie that says, "Unless you have the right look, you'll never be worth anything, you'll never accomplish anything, you'll never be *somebody.*"

Wait a second. I want people to like me. I want boys to like me. And the only way to get boys to like me is to be pretty and thin—sexy. That stuff is important.

Sure, there's nothing wrong with wanting to look good or be liked. But there's something wrong with thinking that how you look or how popular you are is the most important thing in the world, the thing that defines who you are and gives you value. Suddenly you start thinking that without those two-hundred-dollar jeans you'll just die. Or that you have to lose fifteen pounds before you can like yourself. You get into a constant pursuit of more stuff, a better body, and more popularity. A pursuit that'll never satisfy because it never ends.

It's so easy to start thinking that being attractive is the only thing that matters. You forget that being kind and funny and smart and faithful to God are good things too. You start thinking that how you look is who you are. That's how Jessica felt when she wrote to me and said, "I am ugly! I hate how I look. I hate how I dress. I hate my stomach. I hate my nose. Why can't I be different? Why did God make me this way? What was he thinking?"

I bet you've said or felt pretty similar things. Just think about how much time you've spent standing in front of the mirror, saying, "I hate how I look." Or looking at a picture of some famous actress or model and thinking, "Why can't I be as perfect as her?" Soon all you're thinking is "I'll never be pretty enough. I'll never be sexy enough. I'll never be... *enough*."

take a break

Make a list of five things you don't like about yourself.

1. I'm not skinny

2. I have to wear makeup to be pretty.

3. I have TONS of freckles

4. I'm not pretty

5. I have dark circles

Make a list of five things you do like about yourself.

1. I'm a child of God

2. I'm encouraging

3. I'm a good student

4. I'm a good athlete

5. I'm brave

I feel fairly sure you were able to finish the first list a lot more quickly than the second. Why? Why's it so easy for you to make a laundry list of things you don't like about yourself, while it takes you ten minutes to think of even one or two things you do like?

Aren't you exhausted? Hating yourself is a tiring job. And chasing after impossible perfection will wear you out. Don't you wish you could just be liked for the things that are good about you instead of always trying to change?

Sure, that'd be great—if there was anything good about me. I don't see one thing that's good. Nothing. And no one else does either.

Don't be so sure.

All that horrible stuff you think about yourself may be easy to believe. But none of it's true. You're right if you think you'll never meet the world's standards. You won't. Those standards are impossible to meet. They set you up to fail. But God's standards set you up to win. He *wants* you to feel like you're enough, and he wants to help you do it. God knows the real story about you. He sees you for who you really are and for who you can be.

He knows:

- your greatest struggles
- your disappointments
- your home life
- your fears
- what you're thinking right now
- the choices you regret
- what you do in your private world
- what you hope for
- what you dream of

God knows absolutely everything about you. And when he looks at you, he sees your beauty and potential. Not your so-called imperfections. He wants to make you complete, just as he created you to be. He wants to make you see that being you is a good thing.

How God Sees You

Okay, the stuff I said about how God sees you, it sounds nice, but I don't think you're buying it yet. Are you?

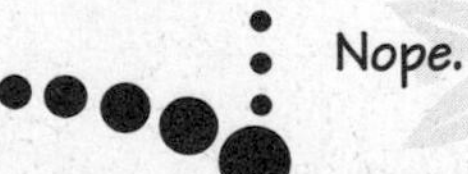

Didn't think so. But seriously, if you believe the Bible is God's Word, you've got to believe what it says, right? So if you don't believe me, maybe you'll believe him.

Take a look at what God wants to tell you about how he sees you.

1. God sees you as beautiful.

Think of the gorgeous beaches those perfect California teenagers hang out on. Or the flowers you hope a guy will give you one day. Or the stars you wish on sometimes at night, halfheartedly hoping that wish'll change things. The stars, the beach, the flowers—God created each of them exactly as he wanted them to be. And each is uniquely remarkable. But of all God's wondrous creations, he gave your creation the most attention. And when he created you, he didn't make a mistake.

Oh yes, you shaped me first inside, then out;
 you formed me in my mother's womb.
I thank you, High God—you're breathtaking!
 Body and soul, I am marvelously made!
 I worship in adoration—what a creation!
You know me inside and out,
 you know every bone in my body;
You know exactly how I was made, bit by bit,
 how I was sculpted from nothing into something.
Like an open book, you watched me grow from
  conception to birth;
 all the stages of my life were spread out before you,

The days of my life all prepared
before I'd even lived one day. (Psalm
139:13–16, MSG)

Um, excuse me. He didn't make a mistake? You've got to be kidding. I'm a walking mistake with all my fat and zits and my ugly hair and big nose.

Okay, that's fair. Knowing that God lovingly created you doesn't change the fact that you have pimples or a nose you don't particularly care for or a million other features you think are unappealing. And just because you're reading this chapter doesn't mean that tomorrow you'll wake up, look in the mirror, and fully love what and who you see. But—and this is a tough skill to master—you have to learn to look at yourself with God's eyes and not your own. Your eyes have been trained by the world around you to see all your physical flaws—and nothing else. But God's value system is different and—believe it or not—better.

Learning to see yourself as God sees you is about learning to look beyond the things you don't like and realizing you've been created exactly the way he wanted. To him, you're unique. And he has an amazing plan for your life that requires zits and a big nose to make it complete. (I know this sounds crazy, but try to trust me.) You can't see it yet, but God has a reason behind every "flaw" and a purpose behind every imperfection.

If you believe what that psalm says, then you believe that God had good intentions when he made you. And he knew everything that was going to happen to you before you were even born. He even knew about the bad haircut you got last week. Every time he looks at you, he sees your life from beginning to end, and he sees how each piece fits together to make something awesome. All you can see is what's in the mirror today. But that's just one tiny, tiny step in God's big plan for you. And he never stops working to make that big plan a reality.

the *Truth*

He who began a good work in you will carry it on to completion until the day of Christ Jesus. (Philippians 1:6)

God started something good when he made you. And having a few flaws doesn't mean he's given up on what he's started or that he messed up in the first place and didn't realize it. You are exactly how he made you to be, and if you can learn to look at yourself with his eyes, you'll see what a beautiful job he did.

2. You are God's mirror.

God created people in his own image,
God patterned them after himself. (Genesis 1:27, NLT)

What do you think it means to be God's mirror in your world?

Being God's mirror means you have the ability to actually reflect the character of God in how you live your life—as you think, act, reason, discern, talk, and interact with others. This means that when others see you, they see God.

Think about how differently you'd feel if you looked in the mirror and saw God staring back at you. You might like yourself a little more, right? It's important for you to understand that you are created in God's image, because this knowledge gives you a basis for your own self-worth. Knowing that God shared his own traits with you proves how much he thought of you when he created you. You may not like who you are. You may not feel very valuable. But God believes your value is immeasurable. He wouldn't give you the responsibility of reflecting his image to the world unless he thought you were worthy of the task.

3. God sees you as good.

Look at what God says about *you* in Genesis 1:31:

> God looked over everything he had made;
>   it was so good, so very good! (MSG)

In this passage of Scripture, God has just finished creating all things. And what is his first response? "It is good!" In other words, he's saying, "I'm pleased with *all* I've made." And, yes, that includes you.

Because his creation of you is good, you have the ability to be good, do good, and thus live a life that reflects him. Knowing you are good in God's eyes should give you a lot to smile about. The world says your significance and self-worth are determined by a lot of external factors, like popularity, wealth, status, sex appeal, and beauty, to name a few. But there's no greater honor and basis for self-worth than to have God say, "You are good."

take a break

Now that we've come a little further, try writing some of your good characteristics again. Maybe they'll come to you a little quicker this time. Then, beside each characteristic, write how you can use it to honor God with your life.

1.

2.

3.

4.

5.

How awesome it is to know that God, the Creator of all things, looks at you and says, "You are good"!

Whoop-di-doo. I'm good. That's nice to know. Now I can just forget about all the mistakes I've made and all the stuff I've screwed up, huh? It's that simple, I guess.

All right, I sense that sarcasm. I said that God thinks you're good, not perfect. He knows you're going to mess up sometimes. You're good because you were made in his image, so with his help, you can be a lot like him. And you're good because, when you accept Christ into your life, his spirit lives in you. Romans 8:26 tells us, "The Spirit helps us in our weakness." So you may mess up, and you may feel like so much is missing from your life, but the Spirit of God fills all those holes and makes you strong where you're weak.

What the Spirit can do:

1. Sanctify you—which means you're made holy and freed from sin (1 Corinthians 6:11)
2. Give you hope (Romans 15:13)
3. Give you special gifts, like wisdom and knowledge (1 Corinthians 12:8–11)
4. Transform you into God's likeness (2 Corinthians 3:18)
5. Give you the promise of eternal life (2 Corinthians 5:5; Galatians 6:8)

God wants you to know he's on your side, no matter what stage of life you're in, no matter what mistakes you've made in the past.

God wants you to know you were made for more—more than just getting by, settling, or giving in. Before you drew your first breath, God knew you. And ever since, he has had his hand on every aspect of your life. He knows you better than you know yourself, and he even knows things *you* don't know about yourself. The Bible says, "Even the very hairs of your head are all numbered" (Matthew 10:30). Think about that the next time you're dyeing your hair black or cutting it all off. Because God created you, he knows what's best for you. And only he can complete you.

My Space

Write a prayer to God asking him to do whatever he needs to do in your life to make you feel complete.

Write a prayer asking God to help you see yourself as he sees you. Then ask God to help you live out the life he would have you live.

Chapter 3

Playing Hide-and-Seek with God

Maybe it's time to stop running away.

When I was a kid, I loved to play hide-and-seek. My older brother and I would play it for hours, and we learned to get very creative when finding a place to hide. I remember one time finding what I thought was the perfect hiding place—so perfect my brother never found me. At least that's what I thought.

After hiding for more than forty-five minutes, I eventually decided to come out of my hiding place and gracefully let him surrender and admit the fact that his younger brother was the best hider. That is, until I found him watching TV in the living room. He wasn't even looking for me. Cheap trick.

I'm a lot older now, but I still play that kids' game. My little girls love to play hide-and-seek, especially my youngest, Brynnan. Except she doesn't fully understand the game. When I get done counting to ten, I shout, "Ready or not, here I come!" And it never fails that I find her facing a corner, standing in full view, covering her face with her hands. She can't see me, so she assumes I can't see her either.

Hide-and-seek is a game of pursuit. The rules are simple: Someone hides. Someone pursues. Believe it or not, the game of hide-and-seek has been around for a long time, actually since the beginning of time. The first couple to call earth home played the game. Except, for them, it wasn't a game at all. It was real life. And the stakes were extremely high. Their choice to hide set in motion a pursuit, not only of them but of all humankind—a pursuit by God.

As you become a woman, it's important that you clearly understand this: you're being pursued—and it's God who's pursuing you. Ever since sin number one was committed on earth, God has been in pursuit of every person who's walked this planet. And he's pursuing you because he wants a real relationship with you.

In the last chapter, I said that the real you, the person God made you to be, is defined by three important things: being God's mirror, goodness, and beauty.

When you read that list, did you want to run to God or hide from him? Were you ashamed because you haven't lived up to God's expectations? Maybe you thought, *God made me to bear his image, but all I do is make him look bad.* Or *God made me to be good, but I've done so many bad things.* Or *I'm so ugly God couldn't possibly love me or think I'm beautiful.*

Feeling like you've let God down or you're not good enough for him can make you ashamed—of how you look or what you've done or haven't done. It can make you believe you don't deserve to have a relationship with him. That shame can make you want to hide from him. But you can't hide from God. And you shouldn't feel like you need to.

• • • • the real deal

Your existence, value, and purpose as well as God's plan for your life are important enough for him to pursue you.

YOU CAN'T HIDE FROM GOD

Let's check out the story of the first humans who walked planet earth and connect the dots to see how their story set in motion God's pursuit of you. The Bible tells us in Genesis that the Garden of Eden was an awesome place to live. A modern-day Garden of Eden would be like having a closet full of the best clothes and the cutest shoes, never having a bad hair day, always getting good grades, and hitting the snooze button as much as you want, all wrapped into one. Oh, and there'd be no sadness or murder or insecurity or self-hatred—there'd be no pain at all. In short, Adam and Eve had everything they could ever want and more. God provided for their every need. But he had one rule: "Don't eat from the tree of the knowledge of good and evil." However, they did exactly what God said not to do.

> The serpent was clever, more clever than any wild animal GOD had made. He spoke to the Woman: "Do I understand that God told you not to eat from any tree in the garden?"
>
> The Woman said to the serpent, "Not at all. We can eat from the trees in the garden. It's only about the tree in the middle of the garden that God said, 'Don't eat from it; don't even touch it or you'll die.'"
>
> The serpent told the Woman, "You won't die. God knows that the moment you eat from that tree, you'll see what's really

going on. You'll be just like God, knowing everything, ranging all the way from good to evil."

When the Woman saw that the tree looked like good eating and realized what she would get out of it—she'd know everything!—she took and ate the fruit and then gave some to her husband, and he ate. (Genesis 3:1–6, MSG)

Adam and Eve didn't realize it at that moment, but their choice to disobey God and buy the lie that Satan sold them set in motion a ripple effect that has continued to this day: *sin.* Their sin separated us from God. And the pursuit began.

take a break

Imagine you're standing on a beach holding a glass of water. Just as you're about to take a drink, a large wave rushes over your feet, you lose your balance, and you spill your water into the ocean. Is it possible to reach down and refill your empty glass with exactly the same water that was spilled? Of course not. No matter how many times you tried, you'd never be able to get that exact glass of water back. You'd never be able to return it to its original state. In the garden, Adam and Eve's disobedience to God had the same effect as you spilling your water in the ocean. That first sin completely washed away God's perfect world and humankind's perfect fellowship with him. We can never restore that relationship to the way it was. But, luckily, God can.

When they heard the sound of GOD strolling in the garden in the evening breeze, the Man and his Wife hid in the trees of the garden, hid from God.

God called to the Man: "Where are you?"

He said, "I heard you in the garden and I was afraid because I was naked. And I hid." (Genesis 3:8–10, MSG)

Why do you think Adam and Eve tried to hide from God?

They were exposed - Physically + spiritually.

As the story goes, after bringing sin into the world, Adam and Eve "realized they were naked" (NIV). Though this is definitely not a funny story, I do find it kind of humorous that two adults covered by nothing more than a few leaves from a tree actually thought they could hide from God. Imagine how silly they must've looked to all those animals, running around naked in the garden, frantically looking for a leaf and a place to hide. This was the first game of hide-and-seek that was ever played. But did Adam and Eve really believe they could succeed in hiding from God?

It's as if they were playing hide-and-seek like my daughter Brynnan, when she stands in a corner and hides her face. Adam and Eve assumed that since they couldn't see God, God couldn't see them either. But he could.

Adam and Eve's response—to run and hide—is so similar to how a lot of people respond today. We mess up. We ignore it, deny it, or try to cover it up. We hope that God will just forget about it or that maybe he didn't even see our sin at all. But make no mistake—God is an all-knowing God. There's nothing you can hide from him—and nothing he's not willing to forgive. As God is making you into the woman he wants you to be, you need to understand that he sees all and knows all. Nothing—*absolutely nothing*—gets past him.

In the Garden of Eden, what got Adam and Eve in trouble? Was it:

Satan?

the fruit?

rules?

their choice to sin?

Only God's Clothing Fits

After their choice to disobey God, look at what Adam and Eve did next.

> Immediately the two of them did "see what's really going on"—saw themselves naked! They sewed fig leaves together as makeshift clothes for themselves. (Genesis 3:7, MSG)

God's original plan for people didn't involve clothing. That's a pretty weird thought for most people because we're so into our name-brand clothes we wouldn't know what to do without them. (But not having to wear clothes would cut down on the time it takes to get ready in the morning, wouldn't it!) Clothes weren't necessary until Adam and Eve sinned and understood what being naked was. Then they thought they could adequately clothe themselves without God's help. But they were wrong. They committed the first fashion blunder on planet earth.

Did you notice what kind of clothing the Bible says Adam and

Eve made? Genesis says their attempt at fashion design was nothing more than "makeshift clothes."

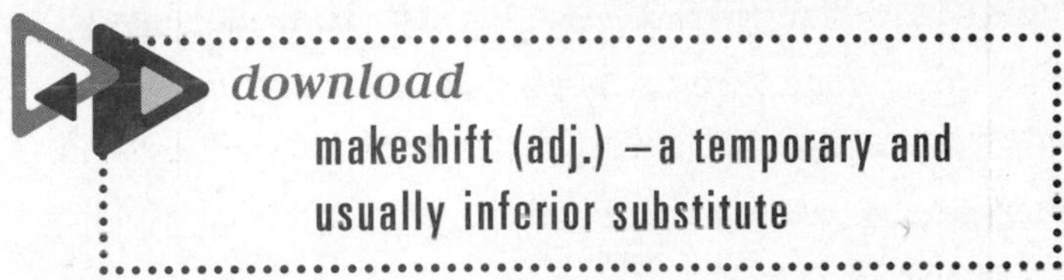

Just about the last thing we'd do these days is make our own clothes. But, just like Adam and Eve, we do try to create our own ways of solving problems without asking God for help. The important point to grab here is not necessarily the type of clothing they made but the idea that whenever we attempt to replace God's plan with our own, the end result will never last and never satisfy. It'll only be a temporary and inferior substitute.

Adam and Eve's first response, rather than running to God, was to run to the world for a quick fix. Isn't this a typical response for us too?

Your Temptation:		**Your Makeshift Clothes:**
There are overwhelming circumstances.	·····	You turn to a drink.
Temptations seem too difficult to control.	·····	You cut yourself.
Everyone else seems to be doing it.	·····	You become sexually active.
You want to be popular.	·····	You try to become It.
You want his attention.	·····	You do *whatever*'s necessary to get it.

I still remember meeting Cassidy in the hallway after speaking to the student body in her Delaware school. We talked, I gave her my e-mail address, and she said she'd stay in touch. The following week she wrote, "I am sleeping with my boyfriend." She told me she couldn't remember the last time she'd read her Bible or even talked with God, and she even admitted that in recent months she'd been exploring the neopagan religion Wicca.

Cassidy was hiding. She didn't know it, but in her attempt to cover up the guilt of her sex life, she was running from God by clothing herself in a Wiccan religion and a sexual relationship, both of which contradicted God's Word.

Adam and Eve responded to their choice to sin just like Cassidy. And the game of hide-and-seek began. But what they didn't know was that there was no way they could ever win. They believed that their makeshift clothing would hide the reality of their sin. But whenever we try to take matters into our hands and rely on the world's help, we always lose.

think about it

- Are you hiding behind an inferior substitute now?
- Is God asking something of you that you're not willing to do?
- Are you embracing something in life that's not pleasing to God?
- Are you in a relationship that's not honoring God?
- Do you have a habit or addiction that's pulling you farther away from God?

For now, *it* may seem to be working.

That *thing* may satisfy you today.

He may make you feel good.

It may seem cool to be *It* right now.

But embracing anything other than God's plan for your life will eventually leave you disappointed and unsatisfied.

God has created you for a specific reason. He has a plan for your life. Attempting to find and live out this plan on your own will leave you with nothing more than an inferior substitute that'll eventually fail you, and you'll find yourself running from one leaf of life to the next. Are you wearing makeshift clothes? God wants to dress you in something much better.

Who Are You Wearing?

After Adam and Eve's initial sin, God could've chosen any number of options:

- End time on earth.
- Kill Adam and Eve.
- Start over with new humans.
- Remove every human's ability to choose.
- Leave Adam and Eve to run around naked until their rears were sunburned.

Once sin occurred, God knew it was only a matter of time before it would happen again. And since humans had free will to choose, God also knew that if he allowed life to continue on earth, every human would have the ability to choose not to love him in return. He could have said, "These humans will never get it right! I should just destroy them before it gets worse." But look at verses 8–10 again and see what God did instead:

> When they heard the sound of GOD strolling in the garden in the evening breeze, the Man and his Wife hid in the trees of the garden, hid from GOD.
>
> GOD called to the Man: "Where are you?"
>
> He said, "I heard you in the garden and I was afraid because I was naked. And I hid." (Genesis 3:8–10, MSG)

What did God do? He went looking for them. He pursued them. Even though they failed him, he still went after them. And then look at what he did next:

> The LORD God made garments of skin for Adam and his wife and clothed them. (Genesis 3:21)

He didn't just pursue them. Once God found them, he clothed them. And he didn't just clothe them. Look at *how* he clothed them—in skin. Some translations of the Bible use the word *leather* here. The point is, Adam and Eve failed God miserably, and what did he do? He didn't just clothe them with any marked-down, half-price, last year's look. He dressed them in the finest clothing of the day. Though they deserved to die, God took care of them by making real clothes to replace their makeshift ones. I guess you could say God was the first designer on earth. What God did for Adam and Eve has *everything* to do with what he wants to do in your life. One thing we all have in common with Adam and Eve is that we're all sinners. God knows this. But regardless of your imperfections, God wants to capture you and clothe you in his finest by making you into the woman he knows you can be, not a woman who settles for an inferior substitute.

Seeing Past the Sin

Imagine how my daughter would feel if she ran off to hide and I didn't go after her. It'd probably break her heart, wouldn't it? But I'd never do that to her, because I love her. I'd never abandon her and treat her that way. The same is true with God.

After the first sin was committed, God knew what was in store. He knew that once sin entered time on earth, life would never be the same.

2 Sins + 2 People = Sin for All People

But an all-knowing God saw the bigger picture. He saw the potential in every one of us. Even though humanity's choice to sin broke God's heart and separated us from him, it didn't separate us from his love. God loved humankind so much that he was willing to allow life on earth to continue. Rather than destroy all people, he set into motion a plan that could bring us back to him. The Bible is the story of God's pursuit of us all. This pursuit brought God to earth in his Son, Jesus. Jesus's perfect life, death, and resurrection make it possible for us to be captured by God and forgiven of our sins, if we choose.

The day you were born into this sinful world and drew your first breath, God began his pursuit of you. He's pursuing you every day because he sees you for the woman you can be—he sees past your sin to the real you. Sure, he knows you're not perfect. He knows you'll fail him sometimes. But he also knows that his plan for you is far greater than your ability to mess up that plan.

take a break

Did you really let this info soak into your brain? If not, listen up. In spite of everything you've ever done wrong, God's still on your side. He's pursuing you. You're so important to him that in spite of the junk in your past, he has an awesome future for you. Just like the two naked runners in Genesis, you've probably failed God. And what does he think about that? He says, "I'm more interested in making you into the woman I can use tomorrow than I am in the woman you were yesterday."

You Don't Have to Run Anymore

Remember Cassidy's story a few pages back? I told her she didn't have to keep running. I told her that God knew about every choice she'd ever made and still loved her. I told Cassidy that even though she'd messed up in her past, God was still pursuing her and wanted a relationship with her. Cassidy stopped running that day, and she asked God to change her life.

Are you running? Maybe you are and you don't even know it—running from who you are, who you can be, or who you know God wants you to be. Eventually you'll run out of steam, out of breath, and out of places to hide. And then what'll you do?

The pursuit began in the Garden of Eden, and it continues to this day, in Cassidy's life and in yours.

To be captured, you have to be willing to trust God. To fully trust him, you must first be honest with yourself.

take a break

Can you remember a time when you've prayed a prayer and invited Jesus into your heart? Romans 10:13 says, "Everyone who calls on the name of the Lord will be saved." If you haven't, you can do that right now. Stop and pray this prayer:

> Dear God,
> I believe in you. I believe your Son Jesus died for me and came back to life. I want to give you my heart right now. Forgive me of all of my past mistakes, and take over my life. Right now I give my life to you. Amen.

If you just prayed this prayer, you've now made the most important decision of your life.

the *Truth*

For God so loved the world that he gave his one and only Son, that whoever believes in him shall not perish but have eternal life. (John 3:16)

Just as God didn't turn his back on Adam and Eve and Cassidy, he won't turn his back on you. Even though he knew your potential to sin, God still created you. His love for you is so great, he was willing to take that gamble. Before you were even born, God saw you as the woman you're becoming now. He wrote your life story before you even started living it. And now he's working every day to bring you into a close relationship with him. The question is not "Is he pursuing you?" The question is "Will you let him capture you?"

My Space

Are you running? Be honest. Real change can't happen until there's real honesty.

Is there something in your life keeping you from accepting God's pursuit and giving him a chance? Write a prayer now asking God to show you if there's anything in your life keeping him from capturing you.

Chapter 4

True Commitment . . . and Taco Bell

Want to know what you really believe?
Watch what you do.

Maybe the only thing more annoying to a girl than not getting asked out on a date is getting asked by a guy she doesn't like. And asked and asked and asked, over and over again. How do I know? Well, it's true that I've never had to deal with a pest like that. But that's because *I* was the pest.

I remember the first time I asked my future wife, Amy, out on a date. I was so nervous. My question was simple: "Would you like to go out?" Her answer was simpler: "No." I remember being disappointed but not defeated. Because when it comes to girls, my motto has always been "If at first you don't succeed, just pester the snot out of them and eventually you can win them over." So I did just that. Every few months I would ask her out, and every few months she would say no. And this little game went on for about four years.

Yes...*four years.* Finally she said yes. She likes to tell me that she felt sorry for me and finally gave me a chance. *I* like to believe that she finally got right with Jesus (ha-ha).

After more than three years of dating, I decided it was time to pop the question. I had a very romantic evening planned. I washed my car, put the ring in my pocket, and picked her up to go to this extremely hip restaurant in Nashville. You've probably heard of it—Taco Bell. Okay, I'm kidding (even though chalupas would be plenty romantic to me). After dinner, with the Nashville skyline in full view and a breeze blowing off the Cumberland River, I knelt on one knee, told her she was "my everything," and asked her to marry me. Fortunately, this time it didn't take her four years to say yes.

Consider this: During the wedding ceremony, the bride and groom each place a ring on the other's finger. These rings symbolize the joining of two as they become one in marriage. What if I took off my wedding ring and never wore it again? Would that necessarily mean I'm not devoted to my wife anymore? Of course not. The opposite is true too. Even if I wear my ring until the day I die, it wouldn't necessarily mean I'm a devoted husband. The thing that unites me to my wife isn't a piece of jewelry around my finger. It's *commitment.*

Think about that word *commitment* for a minute. What do you think it means to be committed to someone or something?

Here's what I think the word *commitment* means:

Believing in and choosing to live for someone or something.

This definition has a two-part requirement:

1. Belief
2. Choice

In my marriage to Amy, I believe in my relationship with her so much that I choose every day to live for it. This means that in moments of disagreement, frustration, or serious heartache, I'm still committed to my wife because I believe in us enough to live for our relationship regardless of the circumstances. The reason many relationships end and marriages deteriorate is that they didn't begin with a full commitment. There may've been a belief in the relationship. But there was never a consistent choice to live for it.

Do you like it when a guy is totally into you one day and then ignores you the next? Probably not. So if you don't like being treated that way, why would you ever treat God that way?

I guess you're wondering why I'm talking about marriage in a book for teenagers. No, I'm not advocating getting hitched before you graduate high school. (I may be from Tennessee, but I'm not that much of a redneck.) We've talked about seeing yourself the way God sees you. We've talked about letting him capture you. But there's another step: commitment. A good relationship between husband and wife requires commitment. And so does your relationship with God.

Heather wrote me to ask what it means to be a Christian. She said, "A friend of mine invited me to her church. So I went. And I was really confused by a comment her pastor made. He basically said that unless you're a Christian, you'll never go to heaven. I'm not completely sure what it means to be a Christian. I believe in God, but is that enough?"

Heather's comments reflect a pretty popular way of thinking. There are lots of people who believe in God. You most likely consider yourself to be one of them. But believing in God does not necessarily mean you're committed to him. The Bible tells us that even Satan believes that God is real. But it's very clear that Satan doesn't live his life for God.

the *Truth*

You believe that there is one God. Good! Even the demons believe that—and shudder. (James 2:19)

Believe It

Satan knows that if he can keep you from truly committing your life to God, then he'll be successful at stopping you from ever becoming the woman God made you to be. How does he do this? It's simple. Satan strives every day to destroy your commitment by convincing you to believe things about God that aren't true.

What do you believe about God?

Commitment Begins with Believing

To clearly understand this, let's take one more look at the story of Adam and Eve in Genesis, and this time let's focus on Satan's role in the story.

> Now the serpent was more crafty than any of the wild animals the LORD God had made. He said to the woman, "Did God really say, 'You must not eat from any tree in the garden'?"
>
> The woman said to the serpent, "We may eat fruit from the trees in the garden, but God did say, 'You must not eat fruit from the tree that is in the middle of the garden, and you must not touch it, or you will die.' "
>
> "You will not surely die," the serpent said to the woman. "For God knows that when you eat of it your eyes will be opened, and you will be like God, knowing good and evil." (Genesis 3:1–5)

Satan, as the Bible says, is crafty. To be crafty is to "use cunning or trickery to deceive other people." The Bible's clear: Satan tricked Adam and Eve. Okay, let's call it what it is: Satan lied to them. Satan knew what God had just told them in Genesis 2:16–17, "You are free to eat from any tree in the garden; but you must not eat from the tree of the knowledge of good and evil, for when you eat of it you will surely die."

No Belief = No Commitment

Adam and Eve believed God. So Satan slithered into the garden and shook their belief system with a very convincing lie. He destroyed humankind's relationship with God by changing what they believed about God. Satan's the enemy, and he's really good at what he does.

Satan's lies continue to this day. Same song, second verse. He lies to you so you'll believe that:

- "God's plan for your life is a lie."
- "You don't need God."
- "You can do it on your own."
- "It's just sex. What's the big deal?"
- "You deserve to have everything you want."
- "Go ahead and cheat. No one'll know."
- "He loves you. So you should just sleep with him."
- "Wearing really sexy clothes is no big deal as long as you look cute."
- "If only ______ takes you to the prom, life will be perfect."
- "It's your life. Live it however you want."

• • • • Duh, why didn't I think of that?

Satan's behind every bad thing that's ever happened on earth.

Behind every smell, there's a source.

Behind every untruth, there's a cover-up.
Behind every sin, there's an enemy.
Satan is the source, the cover-up, and the enemy.

Satan works hard to change what you believe about God. He knows your beliefs drive your choices and shape your convictions. He knows that if he can change what you believe about God, then it'll only be a matter of time before this change in what you believe will affect how you live. Obviously, this was the case with Adam and Eve. I doubt they woke up on that particular morning in the Garden of Eden, went for a swim with the dolphins, rubbed their fingers through the mane of a lion, kicked back and drank some coconut milk, and then said, "Let's choose to disobey God today!"

Nope. Satan waited for the right moment, and then he moved in for the kill. He told the lie. Their belief system changed. This change affected their choices. And the rest is history.

You may be thinking, *How could Adam and Eve have been so stupid? They had everything they could ever want and need. All they had to do was not eat from this one tree, and they blew it!* It does seem pretty ridiculous, doesn't it? But don't we do the same thing? Don't we want what we're not supposed to have a lot of the time?

God says in Proverbs 3:5–6:

With all your heart
  you must trust the LORD
  and not your own judgment.
Always let him lead you,
  and he will clear the road
  for you to follow. (CEV)

When faced with questions like Adam and Eve, do you seek God's guidance first?

He also says in 1 Corinthians 6:20:

> Honor God with your body.

But when it comes to how you dress, who are you more concerned about pleasing—God or other people?

God says this too in 1 Corinthians 6:19–20:

> Do you not know that your body is a temple of the Holy Spirit, who is in you, whom you have received from God? You are not your own; you were bought at a price.

But do you treat your body like it belongs to God? How far have you gone with a guy physically? Have you let what a guy wants come before what God wants?

• • • • take action

Believe it by believing:

- God does have a plan for your life.
- You can be the woman he wants you to be.
- You can stand strong in a moment of temptation.
- You don't need anyone's approval but God's.

The point is, you and I know right from wrong. Adam and Eve did too. But often, without even knowing it, we allow Satan to whisper lies convincing us that the thing we believe is right isn't always the thing we have to do. This is where the second part of the definition of commitment is critical—the *choice* to *live for* what you believe.

Choose It

The great divide between those who believe in God and those who are committed to him is one word: choice.

Commitment = Choosing to Live for What You Believe

In order to become the woman God wants you to be, you have to not only believe in God but also choose to live for him. Making mistakes doesn't mean you're not committed to God. It's impossible for you to live a perfect life. But it's not impossible to live a committed life. However, that won't happen without *your active involvement.* This means you have a role to play. You, and only you, are responsible for your choices.

take action

Choose it by choosing to:

- Spend more time in God's Word.
- Pray that God will shape you into a woman of true integrity.
- Avoid hanging out with people who live against God's will.
- Get back up and try again after failing.

Unfortunately, Satan knows this too. After the lies have been sold, after your belief has changed, and after the sin is committed, you'd think Satan would be satisfied with his successes. But no. He then gets ready to deliver the knockout punch. Once you're down, Satan wants to keep you there. So once again, the lies begin to fly as Satan invites you into the "neverland":

- "Look what you've done now. God will *never* love you."
- "You'll *never* get it right. God will *never* use you."
- "God will *never* accept you."
- "God will *never* make you into the woman he wants you to be."

And all too often, we *choose* to buy the lies again. We *choose* to believe that we'll never be good enough, never be godly enough, and never become the person God desires.

Is this where Satan has you right now? Just like Adam and Eve, have you bought the lie that God's way is the wrong way? Or because of something you've done wrong in your past, are you trembling under a fig tree, buying the lie that God could never really use you to do something great for him? If so, then you're choosing to allow God's work in you to be halted. You're choosing to let Satan use your past to hold you back and convince you that you can never experience a committed relationship with God.

Critical News!

You've got to understand why Satan works so hard to sell you lies. Satan knows the truth about you. We've already talked about how God sees the real you, but Satan sees who you are too. He sees your potential and your abilities. He knows God made you, and he knows God never makes a mistake. He clearly understands that you've been created for an incredible plan. And he's scared. More scared than a turkey in November. He's scared of the woman you are and, more importantly, the woman you'll become. He knows that if he can convince you to buy the lies, he can keep you from ever becoming the woman God created you to be.

Live It

After trying unsuccessfully for almost four years to get Amy's attention, I could've chosen to give up. Instead, I chose to go get that girl and make her mine. Lucky for me, Amy fell and hit her head and developed amnesia. It was during her recovery that I told her we'd been dating for years. She believed me. And every day I wake up with the fear that today might be the day she recovers her memory.

Just kidding. I might've been desperate, but not *that* desperate. I made the choice to pursue Amy. And pursue her. And pursue her. Of course, God's the reason Amy and I are together now. But the point is, I didn't give up. I was active. I chose to keep going. And thank goodness Amy didn't think I was a stalker. But when it comes to your commitment to God, he won't mind if you're a little stalkerish. You've got to make the choice—and keep making it over and over again. You can believe the lies Satan whispers in your ear and give up. Or you can choose to continue on God's path and take him at his word when he says:

- "I've created you."
- "You're my mirror in your world."
- "You are good."
- "You are beautiful."

take action

Live it by living:

- one day at a time, striving to give God more of yourself each day
- to please God over pleasing a friend, a boyfriend, or yourself
- each day as if it were your last

True commitment to God is all about believing in and choosing to live for him.

Not for the past. Not for what other people think. Not for where you've been or what you've done wrong. But for right now. For the future. For the woman he made you to be.

My Space

Do you have a committed relationship with God?

If not, what's keeping you from being committed to him?

Write down five things you can start doing to strengthen your commitment to God. Don't just do this halfway. Be really honest. Challenge yourself, and seriously evaluate your life.

Write a prayer to God asking him to give you the strength, boldness, confidence, and consistency to do whatever's necessary to create and maintain your commitment to him.

Chapter 5

You Were Made for More

To find your place in the spotlight, try giving it up for God.

Before I was traveling the country speaking to teenagers, I was traveling the country singing to them. Yes, for a while I was sort of a "rock star." I made a couple of albums, had my songs played on the radio, and traveled around singing for crowds of adoring fans (at least I assume they were adoring). I loved it. I had been into music since I was a teenager, and I even went to college and got a degree in my beloved pastime. But one day I felt God calling me to do something else. And I finally answered the call.

You're probably wondering why God would call me away from something I loved. I mean, it wasn't like I was singing songs about sex and drugs. I wasn't doing anything wrong. Actually, I was doing something good. I was writing and performing songs to encourage others to grow in their relationship with God. But even though what I was doing was "good," it wasn't the thing I was ultimately created to do. After many years living the life I *thought* I wanted, I realized I was missing out on the life God had made me for. That was when I started to truly understand what it means to live a life committed to God.

Commitment: to believe it and live it

In the previous chapter we discussed commitment: believing in and choosing to live for something or someone. As a musician, I couldn't have been any more committed than I was. But toward the end of my music career, I learned a critical lesson about commitment:

It doesn't matter what you're committed to if you're not committed to what matters.

Believing in and choosing to live for something or someone sounds really good. But unless the thing you live for is truly worth living for, what's the point?

A critical step for you as you become a woman is moving from:

Living for the Good	• TO •	Experiencing God's Best
Succeeding in life	•••••	Succeeding in your calling
Living for what matters to the world	•••••	Living for what matters to God
Drawing up your own plans	•••••	Embracing his plans
Seeing your dreams come true	•••••	Living beyond your wildest dreams
Using your potential for good	•••••	Exceeding your potential through him
Enjoying a good life	•••••	Experiencing the best life

I'm confident there are lots of good-intentioned people doing "good" things for God while they're missing out on God's very best for them. Plenty of people settle for the good and miss out on his best because they've never stopped to ask God if what they think they should be doing is what he actually made them to do. After years of playing music, I finally came to the point of saying to God, "If you want me to walk away from music, I will." Was it easy? I can't say it was, but it felt right. Because when you do something you know is right, the right thing always has a way of easing the hurt over the thing you're letting go.

the *Truth*

I came so they can have real and eternal life, more and better life than they ever dreamed of. (John 10:10, MSG)

Drink Up

Until you accept God's best for your life, you're always going to feel incomplete. The "good" stuff will only partially satisfy—and the satisfaction won't last. This is the lesson Jesus taught one day to a woman he met at a well.

"Will you give me a drink?" Jesus asked the woman. She responded by asking him, "How can you ask me for a drink?" (John 4:7, 9). (The passage goes on to note that "Jews do not associate with Samaritans.")

I can only imagine the expression that must have been on this woman's face. She probably came to this well every day to draw water. But this may have been the first time that a man, especially a Jewish man, had talked to her. This woman was a Samaritan. Jesus was a Jew. And, to put it mildly, Jews and Samaritans did not have each other on speed-dial. Actually, they didn't associate with each other at all. Plus, in those days, it was improper for a woman to talk to a man in public. But Jesus wasn't interested in tradition. He was interested in replacing this woman's good with his best.

Look at what Jesus said next:

> Jesus answered, "You don't know what God wants to give you, and you don't know who is asking you for a drink. If you did, you would ask me for the water that gives life."
>
> "Sir," the woman said, "you don't even have a bucket, and the well is deep. Where are you going to get this life-giving water? Our ancestor Jacob dug this well for us, and his family and animals got water from it. Are you greater than Jacob?"
>
> Jesus answered, "Everyone who drinks this water will get thirsty again. But no one who drinks the water I give will ever be thirsty again. The water I give is like a flowing fountain that gives eternal life." (John 4:10–14, CEV)

Jesus didn't waste one moment, did he? He got right to the point. He saw this woman for who she really was. He saw that she was incomplete. He understood that she was absolutely clueless about God's plan for her life. This is why he said, "You don't know what God wants to give you." She thinks he's talking about a drink of water from a well. Instead, Jesus is talking about giving her a drink of living water—a relationship with him; a relationship unlike any of the other relationships she's been in; a relationship that will make her complete and quench her thirst forever.

In her wildest imagination, though, she would never have guessed she'd go to the well that day and hear what Jesus, a complete stranger, said to her next:

> The woman replied, "Sir, please give me a drink of that water! Then I won't get thirsty and have to come to this well again."
>
> Jesus told her, "Go and bring your husband."
>
> The woman answered, "I don't have a husband."
>
> "That's right," Jesus replied, "you're telling the truth. You don't have a husband. You have already been married five times, and the man you are now living with isn't your husband." (John 4:15–18, CEV)

Wow! Can you imagine? Yeah, it was really bizarre for Jesus to ask her for a drink, but this must have been plain freaky. This guy she's never met before knows everything about her. What's she supposed to think?

Jesus can see she's been trying to do things in her life that were "good" for her. In those days, divorce was usually not the woman's choice. In almost every situation, it was initiated by the husband. And single women usually couldn't own property or make their own living. A woman literally *needed* a husband. So when one husband tossed her to the curb, this woman did what she thought would be best for her—she went looking for another man to take care of her. She didn't realize she had any other choice. But Jesus has come to that well to tell her she does.

What's Your Drink of Choice?

Imagine you're standing in line at McDonald's waiting to get a drink, and behind you stands a man who tells you he knows everything about you. How would you feel? And if he told you he could give you what you needed to feel complete, how would you react?

For years, the woman at the well had relied on the security a man could give her—and every time, that man had let her down. I can imagine she put everything she had into each of these marriages, hoping that this one would work, this time he would never leave, this time it would last forever. But it never happened. She needed hope. She needed a new beginning. She needed to trade what the world said was good for what God knew was best for her. She needed to be complete.

Are you looking for more than just "good"? When you're feeling incomplete, what's your drink of choice? Is it a person? a hobby? a sin? Maybe you find yourself relating to the story of this woman. (Maybe not the five-husbands part, but you know what I mean.) Have you asked God what he wants you to do with your life so you can have his best? Or have you just been doing what you *think* is good?

take a break

Do you believe the life you're living right now is the life God has called you to live? If you don't, write a prayer asking him to reveal his best for you. Then ask him to help you choose his best over all the good things in life.

I bet you're thirsty for something more than you've got. And you may be coasting along, choosing things that are good by the world's standards, thinking they'll satisfy you. Maybe what you've chosen *is* a good thing—it's not sinful or harmful. But you're afraid God will take it away from you if you ask him what he wants for you—so you don't ask. You have to trust that God knows what he's doing. His best will always be better than anything you could've imagined on your own. So how do you really quench your thirst for more? How do you let go of your good and embrace his best? If you're ready to let go of what you *think* you need and grab on to what you *really* need, keep reading.

Thirst Quencher #1: Surrender

Becoming complete begins with surrender. The story of the woman at the well is a story of surrender. The woman had to give all of herself to God before she could walk away from her old way of living and start again. For you, surrender may mean you have to let go of whatever drink you're consuming. Maybe you'll have to let go of something that's become more important to you than God. It could be that there is something in your life, maybe even something good, like a dream, plan, goal, career, or relationship, that you could be treating as a higher priority in your heart than your commitment to God.

Lots of people believe that when you surrender to God, you have to lose all the things that are important to you. Nothing could be further from the truth. The woman at the well's story is proof of this. When she chose to truly let go, she didn't lose anything. She gained everything.

Write down the goals you have for your life for the next five years.

If you could design your perfect future, what would it look like?

question

If God asked you to give up these plans and travel a different road than the one you are dreaming of, would you? Just because you surrender your life plans to God doesn't mean God will call you to walk away from these plans. But if he did, would you?

Thirst Quencher #2: Believe

Dear Jeffrey,

I met you at our camp when you spoke there last summer. I came to camp not really expecting God to do much in my life. I came not even expecting much from myself. My past is

> really sad. I guess you could say that I haven't lived a very good life. But at camp you spoke about believing that God has a better future for us than the past. You said that my past is my past! I believed what you said was true that night. I believed that God could be taken at his word. And my life will never be the same.
>
> Thank you,
> Kelsey

Kelsey chose to take God at his word. She chose to believe that there is a better tomorrow in him—and to *really* believe it. Becoming complete and finding God's best is all about taking God at his word that he has made you for so much more than this world could ever offer.

Satan is so good at selling you lies. We've already established this with the story of Adam and Eve. He wants you to believe that the past, whether it's your choices or those of someone close to you, will keep you from experiencing success in living out God's plan for your life.

But you shouldn't believe that. Every day you have to take God at his word and believe that what he says about your future is true. Check out Jeremiah 29:11:

> "For I know the plans I have for you," declares the LORD, "plans to prosper you and not to harm you, plans to give you hope and a future."

God doesn't say in Jeremiah that he has a plan for you *unless* you've blown it, does he? Nope. He doesn't say he wants to prosper you and not harm you *unless* you've made a mistake. And he doesn't say he only gives hope and a future to those who've lived perfect lives or come from squeaky-clean families. God says he has a plan for you—no matter what.

download

God has a plan for you.
This means that
no matter where you've been,
no matter what you've done,
no matter what your home life is like,
no matter what others think of you,
no matter what you think of yourself,
no matter what your past is like, and
no matter what's happening in the present,
God has a plan for you.

God has a plan for your life. He's customized a unique plan that only you can fit into. You're just beginning the journey of a lifetime—becoming the woman God desires to make you into. As you grow older, God will be able to use every aspect of your life—the good, the bad, and the ugly—to make you into the woman he wants you to be.

He's created you for this exact moment in history. And he wants to use you now to complete his plan. But you must believe it. Because what you choose to do with this moment will determine the *woman* you become.

Thirst Quencher #3: Trust

If you do believe God created you, then doesn't it make sense that the God who created you probably knows what's best for you? And then doesn't it also make sense that if God created you and knows what's best for you, then you'll feel most fulfilled when you fully surrender your life to him?

> Then, leaving her water jar, the woman went back to the town and said to the people, "Come, see a man who told me everything I ever did. Could this be the Christ?" They came out of the town and made their way toward him....
>
> Many of the Samaritans from that town believed in him because of the woman's testimony, "He told me everything I ever did." (John 4:28–30, 39)

The woman at the well moved past just believing and started trusting. She left her jar, went back to town, and told everyone she saw that they needed to know this man too. It's one thing to say you believe in God and that he has a plan for you. To live out that belief is another thing entirely.

What about you? Do you trust God with your life? Do you trust that he knows what he's doing when it comes to you? Are you willing to take a drink from his well and let him make you into the woman he created you to be? If you believe he has a plan for you, you have to trust him enough to choose that plan over any other "drink" you might want.

> The eyes of the LORD move to and fro throughout the earth that He may strongly support those whose heart is completely His. (2 Chronicles 16:9, NASB)

As this verse proclaims, he's waiting to do amazing things with your life if you'll only trust him. Look at what he did with this woman. Moments earlier she was a five-times-divorced, outcast adulteress. Then suddenly she's running back to town to tell everyone about Jesus. The tipping point in her life that took her from incomplete to complete, from good to best, was *trust.*

Thirst Quencher #4: Obey

I have a dog. Her name's Codie and she's pretty special. She's part golden retriever and part chow. Yes, long hair and a purple tongue. My wife and I rescued her from sure death, or at least we like to think so—it makes the story sound more dramatic. We got her from the pound. She isn't the coolest looking dog on the block, but I'm convinced she's the most obedient. I taught her to shake hands, not to leave our yard (and I didn't need an underground fence), and even to open the fridge and pour me a Coke. Okay, two out of three ain't bad. Anyway, she's almost twelve years old, which is like three thousand and something in human years. But after all this time, she still remembers the tricks I taught her, and she still obeys me.

Living "complete" will never be possible without living a life of obedience.

What? Are you calling me a dog?

No, no. It was just an example. I promise. What I was trying to say is that you can never fully become the woman God created you to be until you're willing to obey him in *every* area of your life. Read what the Bible promises to those who obey him:

> GOD will lavish you with good things.... GOD will throw open the doors of his sky vaults and pour rain on your land on schedule and bless the work you take in hand. You will lend to many nations but you yourself won't have to take out a loan. GOD will make you the head, not the tail; you'll always be the top dog, never the bottom dog, as you obediently listen to and diligently keep the commands of GOD. (Deuteronomy 28:11–13, MSG)

What promises does God give in this verse?

- He'll lavish you with good things.
- He'll bless your work.
- He'll make you the top dog. (Hey, that's what it says. Don't get mad at me again.)

But what does this verse say is the key to such canine glory? Obedience.

God promises the very best to those who are obedient to him. Are you living a life of obedience? Don't rush past this question. It's one that deserves your complete honesty and consideration. Does your true loyalty lie with God, or are you just rolling over and playing dead? God knows the truth. He knows if your commitment is to him or to something else.

One teen wrote me and said:

> I always thought that I would follow my dad's footsteps and become a doctor. But lately I find myself wanting more and more to go into full-time ministry. It scares me to think that I could walk away from my dream so easily, and I am not even sure it makes total sense to do it. But I do want to do what God wants, and so I am trusting that he will show me which way to go.

Think about it: Building an ark in the middle of the desert didn't make much sense to Noah. David picking up pebbles out of a stream didn't make much sense to Goliath. Jesus going to the cross didn't make much sense to the disciples. Obedience isn't always about what makes sense.

question

Is there an area of your life you're keeping from God? If so, write it here:

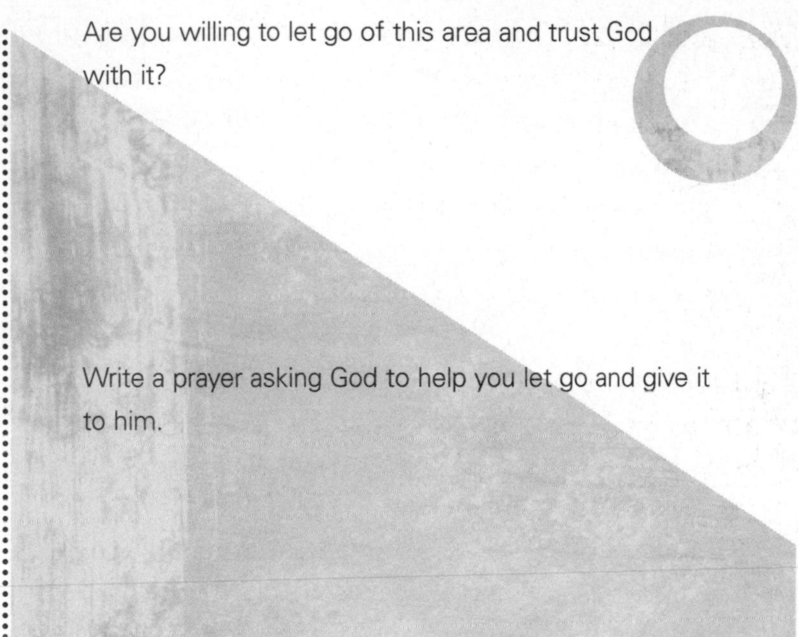

I discovered that when God takes away something, he always replaces it with something better. Sure, there were times when I questioned my choice to walk away from a music career. But I see clearly now that what I did was right. And today I'm experiencing God's very best because of my choice to obey him, even when it didn't make sense to me.

Thirst Quencher #5: Listen

What if you had a friend who called you every night and kept you on the phone for two hours? (That might already be something that happens to you.) And what if this friend never let you get one word in during her rambling about the boy she likes, school, her new shirt, and what Susie told Steve about what Sarah said about Angela? Or imagine if every time you logged in to your MySpace account you couldn't respond to anyone who e-mailed you. What would eventually happen? You'd lose your relationships with these people because the communication would be totally one-sided.

Relationships are a two-way street—talking and listening. There are a lot of Christians who are really good at talking to God, but stink to high heaven at listening to him. And most of the time the "noise" of their life is so loud they never slow down, unplug the life pod, remove the headphones, and simply listen.

John 10:27 says, "My sheep listen to my voice; I know them, and they follow me."

There are tons of voices and noises competing for your listening ear. You have to filter out the noise if you want to hear God's voice.

How to listen to God:

- Make an effort to spend time with him.
- After praying, sit quietly and listen.
- Slow down and give him a chance to get your attention.
- Take off your headphones.

God will never make you into the woman you should be unless you actively try to listen to him. As you begin to train your ear to hear the voice of God, he'll speak into your heart his will and plan for your life. He'll start showing you things you've never seen. He'll lead you in ways you may never have gone before. And he'll challenge you to think in ways you've never thought.

For many years, I prayed to God by going through my list of needs and desires. I'd be very sincere in my requests to him, but I was completely misunderstanding the most important part of prayer—listening.

Are you being serious? I've never heard God speak to me. I just don't think God speaks to people.

Don't be so quick to doubt. First, let me explain what I mean by "speaking." Most likely, God's voice won't boom from a burning bush like it did with Moses. He probably won't open up the sky, send down a dove, and leave a great message, as he did when Jesus was baptized. He's certainly never done that for me. But that doesn't mean he hasn't spoken to me. He's spoken to my heart.

Okay, that's just weird.

Yeah, I admit it sounds weird. But God is God—he doesn't just speak in a human voice. He has countless ways of talking to us through his Spirit. He gives you that feeling inside that helps you make the right choices. (You know, the one you get in your stomach that says, "Don't do it. It's not right.") He warns you when you're tempted, and he sends messages through sermons, songs, and a million other things—if you're looking for them. He doesn't always speak out loud to us—even though he can anytime he wants. Just declaring stuff to us in his "God voice" wouldn't require anything from us. He wants us to really listen and pay attention, to train our ears, hearts, and minds to hear him, so he speaks in lots of different ways.

How God can speak to you:

- in your thoughts
- through his Word
- through a song
- through a friend
- in the stillness of the moment

Do you listen to God when you pray? Or, just like I used to do, have you been guilty of running through your wish list of prayers, never stopping to hear what God wants to say to you in return? At the end of my music career, as I struggled with what mattered to me and what mattered most to him, I started listening to God. And I found out what I should really be doing with my life and what would really make me feel complete.

When you finish reading this chapter, take a few minutes to *communicate with* God. Notice I didn't say *pray to* him. There's a difference between praying to him and communicating with him. Start approaching your prayer life as a time when you communicate with, rather than pray to, God. As you get serious about communicating with God, he'll begin to reveal himself to you. And prayer will be more than something you do just when you need something, or at the dinner table, or before going to bed. It'll become a way of life for you.

Remember, the question isn't "Does God speak?" The question is "Do you listen?"

download

Pray to God: You do all the talking. Communicate with God: You talk. He listens. He talks. You listen.

Jesus took an extreme step to get the attention of a woman that tradition said he could never look at, much less speak to. Satan wants you to believe that God should never look your way, that you aren't good enough to have his full attention. Satan is a liar. God wants to give you all of him. Yes, he knows the story of your past. And he understands your weaknesses. But he looks past your mistakes and sees your potential. He sees you as beautiful. He sees you as his mirror. He sees you as a woman who is good. And only he can give you the best for your life. Only he can make you complete.

To find your completeness, your attention must be on him. Sometimes, like with the woman at the well, God will take extreme measures to get your attention. But he doesn't do this to condemn you. He does it because he loves you. He does it because he wants you to have his best. He does it so you can have water that'll quench your thirst forever. So drink up.

My Space

Look back over the five steps above and consider: Does God have your attention? If not, what steps do you need to take now to give him your attention?

What's the one thing God is asking you to do with what you've read in this chapter? If you don't have an answer to this question right now, take some time to get alone today and download this info into your heart. Then slow down, unplug the life pod, and listen. You just might be surprised at what you hear.

Write a prayer to God asking him to do whatever he needs to do in your life to make you complete.

Chapter 6

Family Funk

Is your family ruining your life? A few hints, and a reality check.

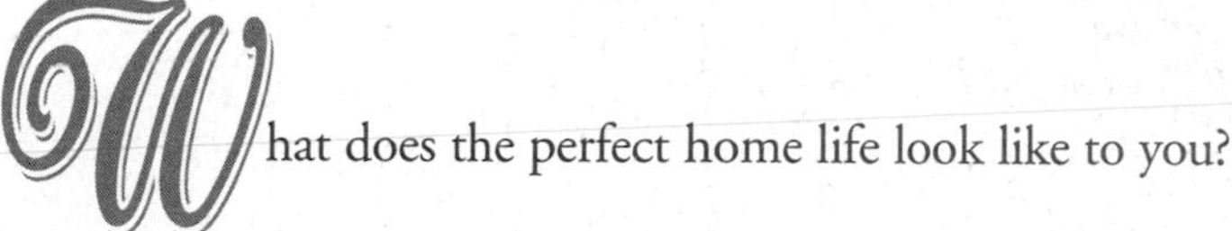

What does the perfect home life look like to you?

Does your home life look anything like your description above? If not, why do you think that is?

Here's what Katy recently wrote to me about her family.

Dear Jeffrey,

My family fights all the time. It seems like no one tries to work things out. My mom and dad fight. My mom is always nagging me about something. And Nicole, my younger sister, and I never agree on anything. I don't want to live like this, but every time I think things are getting better, something else happens and we start fighting again.

Katy

No home life is perfect. I'm sure you have plenty of evidence to support that statement. More often than not, people think things at home are way worse than they actually are. But if you really thought about it objectively, you'd probably have to admit your family isn't so bad. Most of the time, though, it's like you're wearing glasses with magnifying lenses: everything your parents and siblings do, no matter how small or benign, seems huge, like it's just another part of the conspiracy to ruin your life. And you're not crazy—*someone* really is out to screw up everything for you.

What you need to realize is that it's not your family conspiring against you—it's Satan. His plan is to drive a wedge between you and your parents or siblings any and every way he can. And one of the best and most effective ways he does this is by convincing you that your family is worse than any other family. One after another, angry ideas will pop into your head, courtesy of the world's first and best liar:

- "Your parents suck! Your friends' parents are so much cooler."
- "Your parents just don't get you. Forget them. You don't need them."

- "Your younger brother is so annoying. Just ignore him."
- "Your parents like your sister more than they like you."

Family is very important to God. Why do you think he calls himself the Father and Jesus the Son? Why does he call us his children? Because he knows the bond between family members is one of the greatest and strongest this world can offer. So causing problems in your family doesn't just make you and your parents and siblings unhappy—it makes God unhappy too. Your job as a woman of God is to make your family relationships better, not worse. So take a shot at putting aside the things that sometimes go wrong, and let me suggest a few ways you can make more go right in your house.

Getting Along with Good Ol' Mom and Dad

Whether you have one or both parents actively involved in your life, you probably drive each other crazy a lot of the time. Maintaining a healthy relationship with Mom and Dad is not solely your parents' job. If you want to be the woman God created you to be, the responsibility rests on your shoulders too. Romans 12:18 says to "do your best to live at peace with everyone" (CEV).

Recently I was in Texas, speaking to students in public schools. One night during my trip I spoke to parents. That's where I met Pam, a single mother of three. Her husband had left her four years earlier. Her two sons and daughter are teenagers. Pam explained how being a single mom and working a full-time job leaves little time for real communication with her three kids. She explained how her once close family was now falling apart because all of them were busy living their own lives and not paying much attention to each other. Pam was devastated by this.

I offered some possible solutions for Pam to try. However, in this situation, like many, it takes work from everyone involved. For healing to happen in many families in a funk, all family members have to do their part. Your number-one responsibility is to do *your* part—not tell your little brother or sister what to do (even though they may really need it) and not blame every problem on your parents being "unfair" (even though their rules can seem really unnecessary sometimes). So how do you do your part? First, let's look at a few ideas about how to have a better relationship with your parents.

the *Truth*

Children with good sense
make their parents happy,
but foolish children make them sad.
(Proverbs 10:1, CEV)

Honor Them

Okay, let's start with the verse I'm sure you've heard more times than you'd like to remember. Exodus 20:12 says, "Honor your father and your mother." There's no mistaking what God is saying in that verse. It doesn't say to honor them unless you disagree with them. It just says honor them. Period.

Showing honor to your parents is easy on Christmas morning when they're giving you the new cell phone/music player/camera/computer you asked for or money to buy the outfit you've been dying to get. Respecting their wishes when you don't agree with them is a different thing entirely. In that situation, honoring them may not give you the result you're after. But consistently being respectful will show your parents that you're mature enough to obey them, even when it stinks. This'll prove to be to your advantage someday. Take a look:

> Obey your father and your mother, and you will have a long and happy life. (Ephesians 6:2–3, CEV)

Plus, they might let you do more stuff if they see how respectful and mature you can be.

Be Honest

Think back to the last argument you had with your parents. What was it over? Does it even really matter today? If you're being honest, you'd probably agree that most disagreements you have with Mom and Dad begin over little things. But if you're not careful, these little things can start to become big things. When you and your parents disagree, it's important to be honest and on point at the beginning, so small disagreements don't turn into all-out war. When you don't communicate exactly how you feel, you build up a lot of anger and often end up saying something hurtful that you'll regret later.

But it can be risky to be open and honest, especially when you assume the thing you're going to say may not be received too well by your parents. That's why you need to remember these three tips when you're trying to resolve an argument:

1. *Always speak with respect.* Your parents may not agree with what you say. However, an honest word spoken with respect will get you a lot further than an honest word spoken with disrespect.

2. *Never speak with anger.* This may mean that when an argument starts, you need to take time to cool down before a discussion continues. Proverbs 15:1 says, "A kind answer soothes angry feelings, but harsh words stir them up" (CEV). If you really want to resolve a conflict rather than keep arguing, then don't forget this: Speaking out of anger will never resolve a conflict. It'll only make it worse.
3. *Choose your words wisely.* Speaking honestly is important. However, this doesn't mean you have complete freedom to babble on and on just to get your point across. Choose your words wisely. Proverbs 10:19 says, "You will say the wrong thing if you talk too much—so be sensible and watch what you say" (CEV).

Remember: Mom and Dad < Perfect

Parenting is a tough job. And your parents aren't perfect. No one could do what they do flawlessly all the time. But your mom and dad are doing their best, and their best is probably a lot better than you realize.

Have you ever stopped to consider how much your parents do for you? Without even realizing it, you most likely expect one or both of your parents to be a financial manager, housekeeper, personal shopper, launderer, chef, volunteer, medic, counselor, groundskeeper, chauffeur, and hander-outer of cash when you're in need of a financial fix. As if all that weren't enough, they also have more than just you to worry about: your siblings, your grandparents, their jobs, the bills, the dog you promised you would feed but never actually do…it's a long list. No parent could handle all this stuff perfectly, because no parent is perfect. And in case you've forgotten, you aren't perfect either.

So when your parents make you angry, try to remember all the things they do right rather than the few times they fall a little short. I'm sure you'd like them to do the same for you, especially when you're asking to stay out an hour past curfew.

Surprise Them

Amy said the reality hit her during her senior year of high school: soon she wouldn't be living under the same roof as her parents anymore. In her effort to make the most of the time she had left at home with Mom and Dad, she blocked out time one night a week to hang with her parents. Going to a movie, watching a game, working in the yard, or just sitting and talking created lasting memories to take with her when she left for college.

When was the last time you did something special for a parent? Maintaining a healthy relationship with Mom and Dad isn't just about doing everything right in a moment of conflict. Be proactive in strengthening your relationship with your parents. I'm not saying to kiss up to them or angle for favors. But going the extra mile, especially when it's least expected, can do wonders for a relationship.

Surprise Mom and Dad this week.

- Clean up the house without being asked.
- Look around the yard for a project that your mom or dad hasn't found time to finish—and finish it.
- Take your younger brother or sister to the mall or to a friend's house to give Mom and Dad a night to themselves.
- Cook dinner for them.

• • • • Give 'em a heart attack

Believe it or not, Mom and Dad still like to spend time with you. Instead of hanging with your friends, take one night this weekend and ask your mom and dad out on a date. Take them to their favorite restaurant, and eat, talk, and get to know each other even more. And hope that your parents offer to pay.

Silencing Sibling Rivalry

I have two brothers. One older. One younger. Yes, I'm a middle child. And yes, this explains a lot about me. Growing up was never dull in our home. One bathroom, one go-cart, one Atari, and three boys always meant that someone was hoarding, someone was complaining, and someone was waiting in line.

I remember the time my older brother and I painted our neighbors' fence, without their permission. And then there was the time we walked across the top of a waterfall, barefoot, on incredibly slippery rocks, fifty feet above a riverbed. I also recall when we stripped down to our skivvies and water-skied past a boat full of fishermen. That was pretty funny, until I lost my balance and came to a sudden stop on my… Well, let's just say it hurt. We did some pretty stupid—and awesome—things growing up.

We had a lot of fun together, but like all siblings, my brothers and I didn't agree on everything. And a lot of times we found ourselves in some heated arguments, usually about really insignificant things like who got to hold the remote or whose turn it was to mow the lawn or who was going to ride shotgun. There were times when the arguments got really intense, and we would get so mad at each other we couldn't stand it.

But today my brothers are two of my closest friends. And the time I spent with Kent and Jeremy growing up made for memories that'll last a lifetime. The ups and downs of sibling relationships are a part of every family. And rivalries among siblings are a normal part of growing up. There'll be times in even the best relationships when conflicts flare up. But there's a right and a wrong way to handle them.

In the story about the first brothers on earth, Cain, Abel's brother, handled their sibling conflicts completely wrong. Let's see what we can learn from their story.

> Abel was a herdsman and Cain a farmer.
>
> Time passed. Cain brought an offering to GOD from the produce of his farm. Abel also brought an offering, but from the firstborn animals of his herd, choice cuts of meat. GOD liked Abel and his offering, but Cain and his offering didn't get his approval. Cain lost his temper and went into a sulk.
>
> GOD spoke to Cain: "Why this tantrum? Why the sulking? If you do well, won't you be accepted? And if you don't do well, sin is lying in wait for you, ready to pounce; it's out to get you, you've got to master it."
>
> Cain had words with his brother. They were out in the field; Cain came at Abel his brother and killed him.
>
> GOD said to Cain, "Where is Abel your brother?"
>
> He said, "How should I know? Am I his babysitter?"
>
> GOD said, "What have you done! The voice of your brother's blood is calling to me from the ground. From now

> on you'll get nothing but curses from this ground; you'll be driven from this ground that has opened its arms to receive the blood of your murdered brother. You'll farm this ground, but it will no longer give you its best. You'll be a homeless wanderer on Earth." (Genesis 4:2–12, MSG)

What a sad story. Cain made a terrible choice that cost him his brother, his family, and his future. As a woman being made into God's likeness, you're responsible for being a sister who works toward unity, no matter the situation, no matter who's right, and no matter how wronged you may feel.

Love Trumps Pride

The story of Cain and Abel is the first story of many about two siblings caught up in competition. Cain realized that Abel had one-upped him before God. Instead of celebrating his younger brother's decision to honor God and commending him on a job well done, Cain allowed jealousy and pride to overtake him. The end result was devastating.

Proverbs 16:18 says, "First pride, then the crash—the bigger the ego, the harder the fall" (MSG). A woman of God understands that family love always trumps pride. Work hard to be a sister who lifts up your siblings rather than tearing them down.

•••• a little sisterly love

- Be a sister who defends a sibling when they're being criticized or made fun of.
- Keep a sibling accountable for their actions without being critical.

- A younger brother or sister may seem like they're always in the way. But remember, they most likely look up to you, and because of that, they want to be around you. Work to be someone who deserves their admiration.

You're on the Same Team

Family conflicts will never completely disappear. You won't always agree with your family members' choices, convictions, or lifestyles. You need to know that's okay. There's no one on this planet exactly like you, so there's no one you're going to agree with 100 percent of the time. But remember, God has given you your family. It's the only one you've got. So you should take good care of it.

Also keep in mind that in a moment of conflict, rather than fighting to the very end to win, no matter how angry you may be, you need to be a woman who's willing to walk away. Cain wasn't willing to do this, and it cost him a brother and gained him a life of misery. Proverbs 10:12 says, "Hatred stirs up dissension, but love covers over all wrongs." Love can overcome any conflict. Strive to be a peacemaker in your house. In family life, disagreeing is inevitable. But as you're working to become the woman God wants you to be, strive to be a sister and a daughter who promotes love, not anger.

Here are some suggestions to get you headed in the right direction:

Be a Slacker

The next time an argument begins to brew, regardless of whose fault you think it is, step back and take a breath. Most likely the thing that's got you upset will be long forgotten before you know it.

Also, if you're not fighting to be the one who makes an argument first, you will have the chance to listen to someone else. Lines of communication break down because everyone's more concerned with their own agendas than with actually trying to find common ground. More times than not, we fight because no one can button their lips long enough to listen.

the *Truth*

You should be quick to listen and slow to speak or to get angry. (James 1:19, CEV)

It takes real maturity to realize that arguing will never resolve a conflict. This is one of the few times in life when it's okay for you to be a slacker. When in a fight, rather than "fighting to the death," just cut them a little slack.

Check Out the Word

As you continue to grow and mature, you'll start developing your own convictions about your life. When you do, it's inevitable that sometimes your beliefs will be at odds with your parents' or siblings'. When that happens, you need to remember that God's Word never shifts or changes. When you disagree, the best place to look for resolution is the Bible. Turning to Scripture can be a powerful lesson for both you and the rest of your family.

Establish Rules

This one might really freak out your parents, but in a good way. Before you have another one of those wake-the-neighbors, call-in-the-reinforcements kind of arguments, approach your family about establishing a few guidelines all of you will follow the next time you find yourself in a family funk. I've really made this one easy for you. Below is a list of Cool Conversations Criteria that you can take to your parents. Read over it, add a few of your own if you want, and yes, you can copy them onto a different sheet of paper and really impress them with these ideas you came up with "all on your own."

ALERT!

If you haven't carried out such mature procedures before, you may want to ask your parents to sit down before you discuss these Cool Conversations Criteria with them. If they do happen to be standing when you present them with these criteria, allow time for them to get up off the floor before continuing the conversation. Also, be ready—there could be a momentary skip in their heart, loss of blood to their brain, or simply a shock that sends them into hysteria. Remain calm. This will pass.

Cool Conversations Criteria

In a moment of disagreement:

1. Give each person adequate time to talk.
2. When one person is talking, they must do so in a calm, reasonable tone. Otherwise, the conversation should stop until all parties have cooled off.
3. When one person is talking, the other(s) should listen without interrupting.
4. If the argument cannot be settled right then, agree to a time when all parties will reconvene to finish the conversation.

the *Truth*

Don't be a fool
and quickly lose your temper—
be sensible and patient.
(Proverbs 29:11, CEV)

Just Apologize

Have you ever said or done something you regretted later? If you haven't, then you just must not be human. Being willing to admit you're wrong shows you're a woman who's trying to live a godly life. Numbers 5:7 says a person "must confess the sin he has committed. He must make full restitution for his wrong."

This verse doesn't say you only apologize to someone when you've been caught. It could be that, without their knowledge, you've wronged someone by disobeying them, lying to them, or keeping something from them. Your relationship with your parents and siblings will only be as strong as your willingness to maintain honesty. If you've wronged someone in your family, go to them and ask for their forgiveness.

Forgive the Funk

Everyone's family smells at one time or another. And I'm not only referring to when one family member has eaten a double pepperoni pizza. Sometimes family life isn't fun. Sometimes it's unfair. Many families suffer through divorce, abuse, addictions, anger, and abandonment.

Maybe your dad walked out on your family years ago. Or your mom cheated on your dad and no longer lives at home. Maybe one of your parents hits you. It could be that your parents put you up for adoption when you were born, and you've never even met them. You might have a parent who's made it clear they don't want to be part of your life. These are really difficult things to handle, but you can always hold on to this promise:

> Even if my father and mother abandon me,
> the LORD cares for me. (Psalm 27:10, HCSB)

You may have plenty of valid reasons to feel hurt, upset, or even ticked off at a family member. And some problems are too big to be fixed simply by following my suggestions. But it may also be true that your anger, no matter how justifiable it is, is keeping you from living a full, godly life. It may be holding you back.

You'll never have the answers to all the whys: Why did they leave me? Why didn't they want me? Why do they hurt me? There can be so many. You can't control what your parents or siblings have done or will do. But you can control how you choose to deal with it from this moment on.

Check out Colossians 3:13:

> Put up with each other, and forgive anyone who does you wrong, just as Christ has forgiven you. (CEV)

Listen, I know this one may not be easy. And if it seems like life has dealt you a bad hand thus far, I'm not going to tell you that you shouldn't be upset. However, you'll never become the woman God desires you to be if you're harboring anger in your heart. Do you need to forgive someone? If so, take a moment and write a letter of forgiveness to them. You might never show this to them. But releasing your anger can be freeing—even if you're only releasing it onto a piece of paper.

If you're dealing with a painful situation at home, remember: your home life is no surprise to God. He knows exactly what you're going through. And don't forget: God never makes a mistake. He's placed you in the family you're in for a reason. It may seem like hell on earth to you right now, having to deal with your family issues. But don't give up—that's what Satan *wants* you to do. He worked to destroy planet earth's first family, and he'll work just as hard to destroy yours. Your situation may stink, but remember, everything is part of God's great plan for you.

Romans 8:28 says, "And we know that God causes all things to work together for good to those who love God, to those who are called according to His purpose" (NASB).

God has created you for this moment in time. He will cause the story of your home life to help fulfill his plan for you. As God continues to mold you into the woman he knows you can be, you can use the lessons learned through your family conflicts to help others through theirs.

My Space

Take a moment to consider your home life.

1. If there was one thing your family members would change about you if they could, what do you think it would be?

2. What can you do to become a better daughter to your parents?

3. What can you do to become a better sister to your siblings?

Chapter 7

Friend or Fool

How to know if your best friends are actually enemies...and what to do about it.

I knew I was being watched. As I was led through each security checkpoint, I felt more and more of my rights being stripped away. The prison was so cold, so quiet, so lonely that I could almost feel the heaviness of the concrete walls closing in on me. And I was only a visitor. I had always wondered what it was like on the inside of a maximum-security prison. I would never wonder again.

The building was fairly new and neatly kept. However, the evidence of a brutal reality showed on the faces of every inmate, revealing the knowledge that they would probably never see freedom again. When I met Jason, he was still a new kid on the block, in his first year of a life sentence without parole for murder. Jason was nineteen. We talked for a long time about his past, his broken home, a father who could care less about him, and how he grew up on the streets of Baltimore, dealing dope and packing heat before the end of fourth grade.

Jason could've made excuses for where he was. He could've laid blame for his poor choices on his family, his life in the ghetto, or his deadbeat dad. Instead, he looked me square in the eye and said, "There's no one to blame but me. I chose this path. I chose my friends. I hung out with the wrong crowd. Now I'm paying the price."

Before he received his life sentence, Jason never stopped to ask himself if the people he hung out with were hurting him or helping him. He wanted so badly to be cool that he ignored his better judgment when his friends encouraged him to join a gang. He couldn't say no when they pushed him to sell harder drugs. And by the time they got the idea to rob a convenience store, Jason's character was so changed he hardly paused before he said he was in. He didn't consider how wrong it was, he didn't think about what could happen when they had loaded guns in their pockets, he didn't think that someone could die and he could go to prison. But now he has a lifetime to consider all of it. And a lifetime to wish he had chosen better friends.

Friendships. We all have them. We all want them. And, to a certain extent, we all need them. Jason's case is extreme, of course, but your friends are one of the most powerful influences in your life today. But do you ever really think about the friendships you have and how they affect you? Do you put a lot of consideration into choosing good, Christian friends, or do you simply search for acceptance from the most popular, the coolest, or the most exciting?

Who are your five closest friends?

Why are these people your friends? There are probably a lot of reasons:

1. They've accepted you.
2. You have a lot in common with them.
3. They make you feel secure.
4. You trust them.
5. They're loaded!

Okay, except for that last one, all of those are pretty valid reasons. But there's one criterion missing from the list: they need to live godly lives. As you're becoming a woman, you need to think about whether *every* area of your life fully honors God. And your friendships are a huge part of your life. Your friends seriously impact you—how you dress, how you talk, how you act, who you date, what music you listen to, and even how you treat your parents.

I know you're probably thinking, *I don't let my friends influence me like that. I decide what I want to do. Just because I spend time with someone doesn't mean I always do what they do.*

Well, it may seem that way. But read what Julane wrote to me recently:

> Jeffrey,
>
> I never thought that much about the friends I was spending time with before you spoke at my church. But I can honestly admit you were right. When my dad took a new job, we went with him. My new friends, I guess you could say, weren't like my old ones. They drank and smoked and I started doing it too. I also started cursing and fighting with my mom about everything. I never did any of this in my old school. My mom told me I couldn't see those friends anymore, but I did it anyway. I

would lie to her about where I was going so that I could see them. Now I realize that my friends were more than just people in my life. They were people who were guiding my actions.

Julane

Friends = Time

Friends are not just people you know. Like Julane said in her letter, they can be people who encourage or guide your actions. They're people you do *life* with. How much time do you spend with your closest friends? You probably see your friends at school every day. You eat lunch together, talk about boys together, and maybe ride home together. Even if you don't attend the same school, you probably hang out together on weekends, work at the same job, attend church and parties together, chat online, text message, talk on the phone… It's safe to say you spend a lot of time doing stuff with them. Duh, right? That's what best friends do.

Time = Influence

The more time you spend with another person, the more you're influenced by them. That's natural. As you commit time to a friendship, your lifestyle will be more and more affected by theirs. Think about it: You probably watch the same shows your friends do. And maybe you tried out for cheerleading or basketball because your friend was on the team. Your friends do influence you a little, right? But why's that such a big deal? Well, think about this:

Influence = Character

First Corinthians 15:33 says, "Do not be misled: 'Bad company corrupts good character.'" How's your character? Do you find yourself making choices today that you wouldn't have made if not for your friends? If yes, have these choices been honoring or dishonoring to God?

Character = Choices

Make a list of the five choices you most regret making.

1.
2.
3.
4.
5.

Beside each of these regretted choices, write down where you were and who you were with. You were probably with a close friend when you made most, if not all, of these choices.

Friends = Time = Influence = Choices

God knows that friendships are important to you. And he wants you to have truly great ones. But he also knows how much bad friendships can hurt you. So how do you know the difference between good friends and bad ones? Well, unfortunately, your friends are not like bags of Doritos—they don't have labels on their backs listing all their ingredients. However, God has a lot to say to us in the Bible about friendships. In Proverbs 13:20, he gives us a piece of advice that can help in choosing the right kind of friends.

> He who walks with wise men will be wise,
> But the companion of fools will suffer harm. (NASB)

Read that verse again and really think about what it's saying. There are two things I want you to make sure you see:

1. The Promise

The promise is simple: "He who walks with wise men will be wise."

What do you think it means to be *wise*?

download

A wise person: someone who knows the difference between right and wrong and chooses to do what's right.

If you hang out with wise friends, people who know right from wrong and choose right, you're going to get wise. Wise friends will be more able to offer you good advice in time of need, because they believe God's ways are right and they follow them. Simply put, wise friends will help make you a better person.

Do you feel like your friends are making you a better person in God's eyes?

2. The Warning

The warning in this verse is just as clear as the promise—and just as serious. Proverbs says if you hang out with fools, you'll become a fool.

Right? No. It's even worse than that. Look: "...but the companion of fools *will* suffer harm" (emphasis added).

If you hang out with fools, then bad stuff is going to happen to you. This verse doesn't say bad stuff "might happen" or that it "very well could happen." God's word is completely clear. It says you "*will* suffer harm." So if you make the choice to hang out with fools, it's not a question of *if* you'll get hurt, but *when.*

Have you done things with your friends that have hurt you or gotten you in trouble?

download

A foolish person: someone who knows the difference between right and wrong and still chooses to do wrong.

Who, Not What

Notice that the focus of this verse is not on *what* you do. This passage of Scripture doesn't list a bunch of activities that lead to harm, like drinking and driving or cheating on a test or going too far with a guy. Even though all of those choices could lead to serious consequences, the scripture doesn't focus on the what. The focus is on the who—*who* you're with.

It can't get more direct than this. God's saying if you spend time with a fool, you'll suffer. That's why you have to choose friends who are wise by God's standards.

the *Truth*

Fools have no desire to learn; they would much rather give their own opinion. (Proverbs 18:2, CEV)

If you're getting suggestions, support, and advice from friends who don't have God as a priority in their lives, then your life is most likely headed in the wrong direction. No friend on earth knows more than God, and if your friends start acting like they do know more, there'll be no mistaking which kind of friends they are.

Remember one of the Foundational Truths from chapter 1: if God said it, he means it. As you become a woman, you have to be willing to accept God's Word as truth. If it's in the Bible, it's truth. So if you take God at his word, the reality is:

> If you have friends who haven't chosen to live lives that are pleasing to God, then you have fools for friends. And if you keep spending time with them, you'll have to suffer the consequences.

So here it is: are you hanging with the wise, or are you rubbing elbows with fools? If you're completely honest with yourself, the answer won't be too tough. But to help you in this moment of self-evaluation, consider these questions.

Do I have a friend who:

- consistently encourages me to do something that I know is against God's will?

- makes fun of me when I pray, read the Bible, or go to church?
- often lies about her whereabouts to friends or family members?
- encourages me to watch movies, listen to music, or view Web sites that my parents, my pastor, and maybe even I think are inappropriate?
- encourages me to lie to my parents or disobey their wishes?

God wants you to have awesome friendships. He wants you to have fun with good friends. But God also knows what can happen if you choose the wrong friends—which is why He's giving you such a serious warning.

Fools for Friends

So have you figured out if you have a fool for a friend? (If you have, you probably kind of knew it all along, right?) Facing the truth is an important first step. But really doing something about it is what separates the girls from the women. So what are you supposed to do? That's the question Hannah had when she wrote to me:

> Jeffrey,
>
> I know that I have a few friends who are not Christians. And they do encourage me to do some stuff that I know I shouldn't. I don't always agree with everything they do, but if I don't spend time with them, who will share Jesus with them? I'm not supposed to just turn my back on them, am I?
>
> Hannah

Have you ever felt that way? If you've figured out your friend is foolish, you don't want to just drop them from your life without trying to help them. But pointing your friends to Jesus without embracing their lifestyle can be tricky. A lot of times they can end up influencing you more than you influence them. The important thing is to always remember what your goal is: helping them become Christians. Throughout his life, Jesus frequently hung out with people who didn't always do right. But remember, Jesus knew exactly what he was there to do. He didn't just spend time with them to throw a party. He spent time with them for one reason: to show them he was the Savior of the world.

If you know you're in a relationship that's not honoring God, you can still try to witness to your friends without spending so much time with them.

• • • • take a shot

If you're in a friendship that's not honoring God:

- Try to evaluate your intent for the friendship. Is your number-one goal to witness to this person?
- Cut back the amount of time you spend with this person.
- Be consistent in the life you live. How you live will speak much louder to this person than any words you can say.
- Pray that God will give you opportunities to share him with this person.
- Encourage this person to know more about God.
- Invite this person to church, summer camp, or a youth event.
- Don't give up on them.

Be a Good Friend

Jeffrey,

I am the first to admit that we girls can be really mean to each other sometimes. Several girlfriends of mine and I love each other to death. But we also fight a lot about really silly stuff. I want to be a friend that they can count on. But it isn't always easy. One week everything is great. The next there is backstabbing and we're all up in each other's face!

Jamie

Finding and keeping healthy relationships that honor God isn't always easy. But it's an important step toward being the woman God wants you to be.

Strong relationships require a strong commitment. To find good friendships and make them last—and to avoid becoming the fool your friends don't want to be around—you need to remember the following.

1. Be true blue.

One sign of a true friend is loyalty. Anyone can be a good friend when everything's perfect. But it takes a real woman of God to be a trustworthy friend who sticks around even when times are tough. Being someone who's faithful isn't always easy. Loyalty to your friends means that you:

- are willing to defend them
- are willing to overlook their faults
- are forgiving
- aren't going to talk about them behind their backs

the *Truth*

**A friend loves at all times.
(Proverbs 17:17)**

2. Be honest.

True friendship = honesty. Sometimes, in order to be a good friend, you have to be willing to confront your friends about their unhealthy or un-Christlike behavior. Doing this can help them see their real selves by removing the masks that cover their true identities, their fears, or the ungodly lifestyles they may be embracing. A true friend is honest, even when it hurts.

3. Be on God's side.

Romans 12:18 says, "If it is possible, as far as it depends on you, live at peace with everyone." A keyword in this verse is *if.* This word is proof that you can't control the choices of your friends. You can try to be a friend who encourages them to do the right things in life, but you can't control their responses. They may get angry with you. They may resent you. But encouraging them to follow Christ is one of those "if moments." You've got to do it, even if it disturbs the peace. Whether your friends choose to listen or not, *you* have to choose to be on God's side. Be confident. Be true to who you are, even when your friends don't like it or don't approve of it. Be a friend who's on the good and right side, even when others aren't.

4. Be you.

A good friend will never require you to change to gain their acceptance. If you find you have to reinvent yourself to fit in or be accepted by someone, then you're probably not in a genuine friendship. A friend should never determine your choices. And if you let them do this, you're not doing your part to make the friendship the most it can be. Losing yourself in order to be accepted by someone else is never the right way to go. Plus, your friend won't gain anything from the friendship if you simply act like their clone. You should be sharing your best qualities with your friends rather than hiding them so you can fit in. If you've chosen your friends wisely, they'll like you as you are anyway. And they'll be hurt if you don't act like yourself around them.

5. Be a pusher.

Be a friend who pushes others toward a committed relationship with God. Challenge them to spend time with him by reading the Bible and praying. Encourage them to pursue God's plan for their lives so they can also become the person God wants them to be.

> As iron sharpens iron,
> so one man sharpens another. (Proverbs 27:17)

6. Be the good girl.

What's up with mean girls? I don't totally get the mean girl thing, because I'm not a girl, but I do know it's not cool at all. You can't stop all the mean girls in your school from saying hurtful stuff, but you can control what *you* do. You've got to be the one who refuses to respond to their cruel comments. And you've also got to be kind. Girls can be really horrible to each other, sometimes without even realizing it. So you've really got to pay attention to how you treat others. Don't make fun of girls' clothes or laugh at them because they don't fit in. There'll be enough people doing that. Instead, be the girl who shares God's goodness.

7. Be God's friend.

If you haven't figured this one out yet, wake up! Every topic discussed in this book *always* points back to God. The best way to be a good friend to others is to learn from the One who wrote the book on friendships. Just as your earthly friendships require time, you can't learn from God until you commit time to him. When it comes to being a good friend to others, your allegiance to God must come first.

Remember, life isn't about acquiring as many friends as you can. Proverbs 18:24 says, "There are 'friends' who destroy each other, but a real friend sticks closer than a brother" (NLT). Rather than competing to be everybody's friend, be wise in choosing a few close friends you can do life with. Meaningful friendships don't always come easy. And there'll be times when distinguishing between healthy and unhealthy friendships will be hard. But as you commit to stay in consistent communication with God, he'll give you wisdom to know the difference.

My Space

1. Do your friends push you closer to God or pull you away?

2. Do you have friendships with fools? If so, what are you going to do about it?

3. What characteristics do you look for in a true friend?

Write a prayer asking God to bring you true friendships that honor him. Ask God to grant you wisdom to choose good friends and courage to walk away from those who'll separate you from him.

Chapter 8

Dating.com

Can you get close to boys without getting crushed? Here's help.

"Find the perfect date in your area now!"

"Enter your e-mail address and sign up to meet the guy of your dreams!"

"This is where every single person finds love!"

"Get in on the action. Find true love now!"

These are actual ads I found while surfing several online dating services. (No…I'm *not* looking for a date.) All guarantee fast and easy access to the perfect guy. If only it were so simple. And a lot of these sites seem to be more about sex than dating, with suggestive pictures and even more suggestive profiles. But I'll tell you right now, dating isn't about sex, and I'm not going to talk about sex in this chapter.

What? You're going to have a chapter on dating and not talk about sex? That's just stupid. You can't talk about dating and not talk about sex.

Yes, dating and sex seem to be one and the same. But dating is about building relationships and learning to deal with guys. Yeah, sex will come up. But way before you get to sex, you have to figure out what a good relationship is. Dating takes a lot of responsibility—and a lot more time than any of those ads suggest.

Of course, you'd never know it if you took society's word for it. A lot of reality TV shows make dating look like a game or a joke. Just watch them for a few hours, and you'll take relationships about as seriously as you take Paris Hilton. And speaking of Paris Hilton, celebrities, whether in real life or on screen, do a lot to convince us that insanely attractive people run around having sex as soon as they meet someone, get married after a month of dating, and get divorced just as quickly. They *definitely* don't seem to take relationships seriously.

It's no wonder that when I talk to a lot of girls, I discover that even the best-intentioned ones, trying their hardest to live a God-honoring life, are still completely clueless about what dating should really be like. The end result is that many of them have taken a lot of wrong turns and made some big mistakes. What about you? Do you know how to do dating the right way—in a way that honors God?

take a break

If you could plan the perfect date night, what would it be like?

If you've started dating, you might think this chapter isn't for you. Well, you're wrong. You may have a lot of dating experience, but it might not be *good* experience. This chapter isn't designed to condemn you for anything you might've done on dates before but to help you have better, more God-honoring dates in the future.

If you haven't started dating yet, you might think you don't need to read this. Believe me, you do. You need to prepare yourself for what's coming, even if your parents don't let you date now (or if you're still waiting for Mr. Wonderful to ask). As you become a woman, the choice will be yours: dating the world's way or God's way. I really hope that as you read this chapter, you'll examine your dating habits or desires and then apply the necessary changes to let God make you into a woman who honors him in your dating life.

Some say Christian teens shouldn't date at all. I think dating can be a time for you to develop healthy, God-centered relationships with the opposite sex. Dating can cause a lot of problems if you choose to go it alone—without God. But approaching dating from God's perspective will help you develop dating habits that honor God (but still allow you to have fun).

God wants to be involved in your dating life, and if you don't let him, it's unlikely you'll ever really find satisfaction in dating. To become a woman of God, honoring him when you date has to be a priority for you. So here are some dating dos that'll hopefully keep you from stumbling into any of the don'ts.

1. Realize not every guy is datable.

If you could design the perfect man for you to spend the rest of your life with, what would he be like? Make a list of the characteristics your future husband should have.

MY LIST:

Consider the guys you've gone on a date with or want to date. Do these guys match up with your list? If not, why are you dating or wanting to date them?

Read what Shelly wrote me recently about her take on many guys:

> Dear Jeffrey,
>
> Where have all the good guys gone? It seems like every time I get into a relationship with a guy, it never fails that eventually he starts pushing me to do things with him—you know, sexually. Why can't I just find a guy that accepts me and is willing to say no to the sex stuff? That's the kind of guy I want. Do you think there are any left?
>
> Shelly

What Shelly was really saying in this letter is "I want a guy who'll raise the bar. I want a guy who puts what God wants and what I want before what he wants." You may be thinking, *Jeffrey, if I have such high standards for the type of guy I'll date, I'll never go out with* any*one.* Well, it might not eliminate every guy in the world, but it will make your pool of datable guys a lot smaller.

Just think about it, though. What if, rather than raising your dating bar, you choose to lower it? Yes, the number of datable guys has multiplied. But now there are just more unworthy guys to choose from. Just more guys lining up to let you down because they don't value what you value.

Whatever. I just wanna be a normal girl with a boyfriend. I wanna hold hands and kiss and feel like someone actually thinks I'm pretty. I feel like such a loser because I never go out with anyone. I'm, like, the only person who hasn't had a boyfriend—and I just feel stupid.

I know setting high expectations can make you feel like you're missing out on something you have to have. But if you have to lower your bar to get a date, then you're putting that date before God—and nothing should come before him. It's hard because everything around you says you *need* to have a boyfriend, and if you don't have one, then something's gotta be wrong with you. This might be the lie teen girls believe more than any other one. The truth is, having a boyfriend who doesn't meet your standards means there's something wrong with you. Waiting patiently for the right guy makes you smart—and it makes God proud. It's one of the hardest things to do when all the girls around you seem to be jumping from one cute boy to the next. But you'll regret lowering your standards a lot more than you'll regret missing out on some of the junk bad boyfriends get you into.

Take a look again at the list of characteristics you just made of what you hope your future husband will be like. Make a pledge with yourself now to never compromise your list. One compromise will eventually lead to another. Remember, no guy is worth a compromise of your character, convictions, and desire to become the woman God is making you into.

2. Make this one #1 on your list.

There's a question I get asked over and over again: "Is it okay to date a guy who's not a Christian?"

My answer to this question is more questions:

- Would you want to marry someone who doesn't believe there's a heaven, hell, or God, and doesn't believe that Jesus is his Savior?
- Would you want to marry someone who wouldn't embrace reading the Bible, going to church, and praying?
- Would you want to marry someone who wouldn't instill in your children godly character and the practices of praying, going to church, and reading the Bible?

I hope the answer to each of these questions would be a definite no from you. If this is the case, then why would you choose to date someone who wouldn't do these things? I'm not saying you have to think you're going to marry every guy you go out with (he might be a little freaked out if you talk about kids on the first date). But any guy you date should be marriage-worthy. And the first question on the marriage-worthy test should always be "Is he a Christian?"

Look at what the Bible says in 2 Corinthians 6:14–16:

> Don't become partners with those who reject God. How can you make a partnership out of right and wrong? That's not partnership; that's war. Is light best friends with dark? Does Christ go strolling with the Devil? Do trust and mistrust hold hands? Who would think of setting up pagan idols in God's holy Temple? But that is exactly what we are, each of us a temple in whom God lives. (MSG)

This passage is saying that when you choose to unite with a non-believer, it's as if you're setting up a pagan idol in God's temple. That's pretty serious stuff. I mean, God warns us against making idols and worshiping other gods in the Ten Commandments. In this case, opposites do *not* attract.

But what if you could convince a guy to become a Christian after you start dating? I mean, if he really likes you, he'll want to go to church with you and stuff, right?

Dating a non-Christian may seem innocent. You may think that after a while you'll win him over or that it's just dating, not marriage, so it doesn't matter. But this passage warns that you're walking on dangerous ground when you choose to unite (even just for a few dates) with "those who reject God."

You may think you can turn him into a Christian, but it's more likely that he'll pull you away from Christ. People don't change just because you want them to. They only change if they want to. Talk to the guy about Christ. Invite him to your youth group. But don't even think about giving your heart to him until he gives his heart to God.

3. Expect respect.
You can call me old school, old-fashioned, a southern gentleman—whatever you want with this one, and it won't offend me. No matter who a guy is or where he's from, he should respect you.

Now, I could get a lot of flak for this, like I'm being sexist or whatever. Maybe. But what I know is that girls seem to be a lot more naturally respectful than guys. The way our society is, we just don't teach guys to respect girls very well. So that's why you need to weed out the ones who haven't learned the lesson. And there'll probably be a lot of weeding to do.

What *He's* Thinking

Everywhere a guy looks, people are telling him to act like a jerk. A lot of times guys are disrespectful because they think that's how they're supposed to act. They don't want to seem like a sissy. They want to be a "man." This doesn't excuse it, of course, but it explains it a little. Just keep this in mind when some guy is being a real jerk to you. You shouldn't put up with it. But you should also try to help him know that he doesn't have to act that way to be a real man.

If you need a good example of how a guy should treat you, look at John 19:25–27. Jesus has just been beaten, stripped of his clothes, and nailed to a cross to die, and he is gasping for his last few breaths. Yet, at a time when he could be selfishly focusing on himself, look at where his focus is:

> While the soldiers were looking after themselves, Jesus' mother, his aunt, Mary the wife of Clopas, and Mary Magdalene stood at the foot of the cross. Jesus saw his mother and the disciple he loved standing near her. He said to his mother, "Woman, here is your son." Then to the disciple, "Here is your mother." From that moment the disciple accepted her as his own mother. (MSG)

In his final moments on earth, not to mention at a point of extreme pain, Jesus was more concerned about his mother than himself. He wanted to make sure someone cared for her when he was gone. You may've heard people say that if you want to know how a guy will treat you, look at how he treats his mother. That's a good suggestion. The way Jesus treated his mother was the way he treated everyone—he put their needs before his own. Watch how your guy treats the people around him—his parents, his friends, other people at your school—and you'll get a pretty good idea of what kind of guy he is.

Consider these questions:

- Do you ever feel mistreated by a guy?
- Does he ever make you feel dumb after you've said something?
- Do you often say nothing because you're afraid of being corrected?
- Has he ever abused you verbally or physically?
- Does he belittle or make fun of you for going to church, praying, or reading your Bible?

If you can answer yes to any of these questions, then you're probably in a relationship where you're not respected. And if you try to come up with a lot of reasons why the guy shouldn't be blamed for being disrespectful to you—"He didn't mean it," "He said he wouldn't do it again," "I deserved what he did to me"—then you have a bigger problem: you're not respecting yourself.

Any guy who dates you should realize it's a privilege to date you. And he should treat you like he knows it. Remember, you're a person of value to God—a person who is beautiful, good, and entrusted with reflecting his image to the world—and you should only spend time with people who see you that way. Too many girls start to believe they don't deserve to be treated well—but that's *never* true. Think about your list. I'm pretty sure you didn't include something like "I want to spend the rest of my life with a guy who doesn't respect me." So why would you date one?

4. Take control and have conviction.

You may not be the one behind the wheel on a date, but you can be the one who takes control over where the guy drives. A lot of girls I've talked to have ended up in tempting situations because they never chose to take control and have conviction.

If you're dating a guy whose character is in line with your list, then hopefully more times than not he'll also be in line with your convictions. But let's face it: there are times when even the best of guys has a brain freeze—and this usually occurs after he has consumed too many pieces of pizza or downed a little too much caffeine or has his mind on football, music, or Xbox. Really, it could happen anytime. In such cases, his ability to make rational and wise decisions may be somewhat impaired. Okay, maybe it's not that bad, but there may be times when you need to take over the controls and encourage your guy in the right direction.

Sometimes even a great guy ignores what's right and encourages you to follow him down a road you know could lead to trouble. That's why it's important for you to remember your convictions and always work hard to contain a potentially dangerous situation. Even in a relationship founded on godly convictions, there'll be times when you have to take responsibility for what happens next. So stand up for what you know is right. Be ready to take control.

Be a woman of control and conviction by:

- never going to a party where there are drugs and alcohol
- never parking somewhere alone where you'll be tempted to make a choice you'll regret later
- never watching a movie, sitcom, or video that might affect your decision-making process in a negative way

take a break

Have you ever attended a party where there was drinking, smoking, or hooking up? So many teens say to me, "Well, I didn't know it would be that kind of party!" *Whatever.* You can be a woman who rationalizes and makes excuses, or you can be a woman who makes a difference. More times than not, you know what's going to happen at a party. Even if you and your date don't get involved in any of the bad stuff that's going on this time, the more you surround yourself with sinful things, the more likely it is you'll do them sooner or later.

the *Truth*

Do not be misled: "Bad company corrupts good character." (1 Corinthians 15:33)

5. Apply the WWJD approach.

No, contrary to popular belief, WWJD does not stand for "We Want Jeffrey Dean." (Well, maybe it's not a popular belief with everyone, but some people have said it... I mean, I'm sure *someone* has...) Unless you've been living in a cave for the past few years, you probably know that WWJD stands for "What would Jesus do?" The WWJD bracelets were once a seriously popular accessory, but today the bracelet isn't so fashionable. However, the WWJD acronym still represents an essential approach for you if you want to honor God in your dating life.

"What would Jesus do?" Do you ever think about that question when deciding who to date or what to do on a date?

Wait a second. Jesus didn't go on dates.

Okay, it's true Jesus didn't go on dates. But he had plenty to say about staying pure and respecting other people and loving God before anything else—all important advice for dating as well as life in general. So you may not be able to open up one of the gospels and read about a teenage Jesus holding hands with his girlfriend or anything, but you can learn a lot from him that'll apply to your dating life. Developing the habit of asking the WWJD question won't necessarily mean you'll always make the right dating decisions. But trying to approach the dating experience with the mind of Christ will keep you more focused on God's desires and less on yours.

6. Know going solo isn't for losers.

I know a girl who seems like the perfect package: beautiful, smart, athletic, godly…and *single.* One day she'll make the perfect spouse. But for now she's totally cool with going solo. She told me:

> Why rush it? My life is great right now. I'm enjoying high school, sports, and just spending time with my friends. Dating usually just confuses everything, and I'm in no hurry for that.

Going solo is cool. You don't have to date just because you're a teenager and you feel like that's what you're supposed to do. In fact, choosing not to focus on guys frees you up to focus on:

- grades
- sports
- today's nail color
- yourself
- your future
- learning to milk a cow (if you were all alone on an island with a cow, this would be important knowledge)
- family
- college
- today's hair color
- friends
- just enjoying yourself, without all the dating drama

my favorite things to do in life:

And the most important thing of all: you'll have more time to develop your relationship with God. Guys will come and go, and maybe come and go again…and again. But your relationship with God is lifelong. And you never have to worry about him breaking up with you.

Oh, just one more thing. Getting closer to God will also help you know you don't need a guy to feel complete. Only God can really make you feel that way. And the more time you spend depending on him—and not depending on a guy—the more you'll start to really believe that.

7. Cut Mom and Dad some slack.

Have your parents said you can't date yet? If so, you may not agree with them. Yet they're still your parents. And, as the Bible says, "Honor your father and your mother" (Exodus 20:12). (As if you've forgotten that verse.)

Instead of fighting with your parents, trying to convince them they're wrong, or going behind their backs and doing it anyway, why not try another approach: Obey them. Honor their wishes. Rather than defy them, work to prove to them that you're responsible and trustworthy.

I still remember double-dating with my best friend Louis when I was fifteen. Louis and I and our dates rode in the backseat of his parents' car as they drove us to a movie and dinner. I'll admit that, at the time, this seemed like dating suicide. But now I realize that Louis's parents were just out to protect us. Going on a few dates with Louis's parents helped me develop respect for the entire dating process. And once I started dating without a parent on board, I understood what a privilege it was to be given the trust of my parents—and to not be chauffeured around like a little kid.

You may not always agree with your parents' wishes. But keep in mind, your parents have your best interest at heart. If you feel strongly that you're ready to start dating, talk to your parents. Your willingness to discuss it with them respectfully and genuinely will show them you're taking responsibility as a woman when it comes to dating God's way.

And when they let you date, follow through with that promise of responsibility. Only go where you say you're going. Only go out with guys your parents approve of. Come home by curfew. Call if you're going to be late. Don't ever give them a chance to regret letting you loose in the dating world.

don't date a dork

When he picks you up, if he sits in the driveway and honks…let him stay there.

8. Pray before your dates.

Prayer is a critical step to helping you establish and maintain healthy dating relationships that honor God. In Luke 22:40, Jesus challenged his disciples to "pray that you will not fall into temptation."

This one isn't for wimps. I'll admit that a lot of teens I talk to tell me they choose not to apply this to their dating life. Though it may not be a popular point, I think it's an essential one. Because prayer changes everything.

hit pause

Have you ever prayed with a guy before a date?

Why or why not? Does the idea of doing that sound reasonable to you...or just plain crazy?

The next time you start dating a guy, gather up all your courage and try these three things:

1. Pray before he picks you up.
2. At a restaurant, pray with him before eating.
3. As the relationship grows, let him know you pray for him and for your relationship with him.

As the relationship continues to mature, the hope is that he'll see prayer as an important part of your life. The ultimate goal might be that the two of you pray together before you pull out of the driveway. When you do, get ready. Because one of two things will most likely happen:

1. You'll freak him out, and he won't want to go on a date again. If this is his reaction, then most likely he's not the kind of guy you need to be dating. Better to find out now rather than five dates later when you're really starting to like him.
2. He'll show his true colors, proving that he is, in fact, a guy who loves Jesus. And he just may dig you all the more for loving the Lord too.

Praying with a guy on a date may not happen overnight. That's okay. Don't beat yourself up if this is a difficult step for you to take. Just continue to work toward the goal of being a girl who prays with her date.

Praying before a date begins will:

- set the tone for the date
- establish a God-centered foundation not only for the date but for the whole relationship
- send a powerful message to him that you want to honor God on your date

By the way, dating a Christian guy will make the praying thing a lot easier. Heck, if he's a Christian, he might even initiate the prayer. But the thing that'll make dating easiest (though not completely simple, because dating is *never* simple) is to let God guide you in every choice you make.

My Space

Most likely your future spouse is living somewhere on planet earth at this very moment. It's also possible you don't even know him. Remember, I didn't meet my wife until I was in college.

Since it's very probable your future spouse is alive, it's also pretty possible he's dating someone other than you right now. So ask yourself these questions:

a. What standard do I expect him to hold himself to while dating other girls?
b. Do I hope he'll raise the bar of excellence in how he treats her?
c. Do I hold myself to the same standard I expect him to hold himself to?
d. Do I strive to raise the bar in how I treat a guy I date who just might marry someone other than me?

Write a letter to your future spouse, outlining the kind of relationship you hope to have with him one day when the two of you start dating and eventually get married.

Now, make a list of the godly character and qualities you'll exhibit in your dating life with other guys and, eventually, with the one you'll marry.

Make a list of the top characteristics you want your future spouse to have.

Write a prayer asking God to help you and your future spouse stay true to these desires.

Chapter 9

It's Just Sex, Right?

How to keep your cool on a very heated subject.

In downtown Nashville, there's an adult bookstore (which, in case you're wondering, I've never been inside) with a large sign that reads: WHAT'S THE BIG DEAL? IT'S JUST SEX!

Contrary to the belief of this storeowner, and many others, sex is a huge deal. Whether you've been sexually active or not, you've probably at least thought about sex a time or two, or three, or four hundred. But before you turn a deaf ear to this chapter and assume you've heard everything about sex, think about this:

You'll never become the woman God created you to be if you're not willing to surrender *every* area of your life to him. This includes your sex life. There's a lot more to your sex life than just going all the way. And, of all the topics that teen girls write to me about at www.jeffreydean.com, this one tops them all. Check out what several teen girls have shared with me about their sex lives:

"After dating three months, I finally did it. Several weeks later we broke up and the relationship was over. I wish I could go back and change that moment." —Ashley, senior

"Why does it seem like every guy wants sex? Is there anyone out there who will just accept me for me and not expect to get in my pants?" —Amy, sophomore

"I have had oral sex several times. I wish I had never gone that far with a guy." —Amanda, 8th grade

"I haven't had sex. I really want to wait until marriage. It isn't easy. But my parents have always communicated with me about it, and I am determined to wait." —Kelly, junior

Everyone has an opinion about sex. And there's so much info flying around about what's right and what's wrong that it's hard to know what's what. Satan's doing all he can to deceive you into buying a plan other than God's. That's why you need to let God into your sex life. And that's why this chapter is a must for you.

Do you believe sex outside of marriage is wrong?Why or why not?

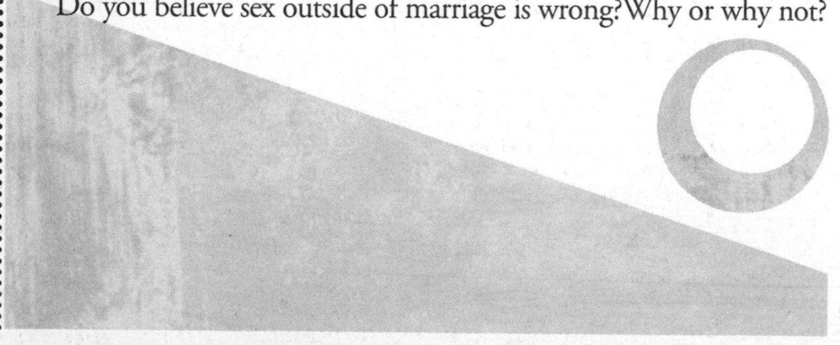

Do you believe there's ever a time when it's okay to have sex outside of marriage? If yes, under what conditions?

take a break

Sex can be an uncomfortable topic of conversation. So before we go any further, let's clear away all the awkwardness. Here we go. Every person (other than Adam and Eve) that's ever lived on planet earth has this one thing in common: we're all here because our parents did it. And before them, our grandparents did it. And before them our great-grandparents did it too (after the five hours it took to remove all those corsets and petticoats and stockings and pantaloons).

Okay. Once the words *great-grandparents* and *pantaloons* have been spoken in the same sentence, it can't get any weirder than that. So the rest of this chapter should be a breeze.

Sex Rocks!

God has created you as a sexual being. And he wants you to enjoy your sex life. I mean *really* enjoy it. Take a look:

Oh, how beautiful!
Your eyes behind your veil are doves.

Your hair like a flock of goats....
Your lips are like a scarlet ribbon;
 your mouth is lovely....
Your two breasts are like two fawns....
Your lips drop sweetness as the honeycomb, my bride;
 milk and honey are under your tongue....
Your stature is like that of the palm,
 and your breasts like clusters of fruit.
I said, "I will climb the palm tree;
 I will take hold of its fruit."

Any idea who penned these lyrics? The author is King Solomon. Yes, the King Solomon in the Bible. (See Song of Songs 4:1, 3, 5, 11; 7:7–8.) Can you *believe* this is in the Bible?

When I think of how beautiful my wife is, I'm not sure "a flock of goats" comes to mind. And if a guy told you your breasts were "like two fawns," you'd probably think he was crazy—or downright creepy. But, hey, it worked for Solomon, I guess. Anyway, weird metaphors aside, this graphic description of two lovers is in the Bible for a reason: it tells us that God wants us to understand that sex is an awesome gift. And when we stick with his plan, sex rocks.

But God doesn't just reveal the sensual side of sex to us in the Bible. He knows that his great gift can be seriously misused. So he's also got some very clear advice for you about sex. Take a look at four words found in 1 Corinthians 6:18:

Flee from sexual immorality.

Let's break down this verse into two parts.

1. "Flee from..."

Obviously you know what *flee from* means—get the heck outta Dodge as fast as you can. In this verse, God doesn't sugarcoat his intentions for your sex life. He doesn't say, "Stop and think about it," or "Rationalize and work to justify it," or "Just don't get too close to it." Nope. He gets right to the point and says, "Flee!" In other words, "Take off! Escape! Put on your running shoes, lace 'em up, and sprint full speed in the opposite direction!" It's clear that God doesn't want you to have anything to do with sexual immorality. But for many, this is where the trouble begins.

In today's culture, "whatever works for you" has become the new definition of morality. It makes it really hard to know just what you're supposed to flee from. The lines get blurred and you can start making mistakes. That's why it's crucial for you to understand exactly what God's telling you to flee. Which leads us to the second part of this verse.

2. "...sexual immorality."

What do you think sexual immorality is?

Sex before marriage seems like the most obvious answer, right? But lots of people (maybe even some of your friends) think that as long as you just don't "go all the way," then everything else is okay.

Yes, in 1 Corinthians 6:18, God is saying, "Don't go all the way."

But if you think that's *all* he's saying, then you're missing God's truest intentions for your sex life. When God says to flee from sexual immorality, he's not just saying, "Don't have sex before marriage." He's saying to run away from *any* sexual impurity.

> But among you there must not be even a hint of sexual
> immorality, or of any kind of impurity, or of greed,
> because these are improper for God's holy people.
> (Ephesians 5:3)

Sexual Immorality = Sexual Impurity

Satan wants you to be confused about God's plan for your sex life. He wants you to believe that the Bible hasn't clearly outlined what's okay and what's not when it comes to sex. He wants you to think there are all kinds of loopholes in God's rules that allow you to do some things that aren't technically "sex." But he's wrong. Dead wrong. God's word is clear: impurity is off-limits.

Sexual immorality = Sexual impurity

Sexual impurity = Sin

No matter the situation

No matter the circumstances

No matter how in love you feel

No matter the emotion involved

No matter how long you've dated

And sexual impurity isn't just about actually being with a guy, doing stuff you shouldn't do. It's also about:

- your thoughts
- the jokes you tell
- the jokes you hear
- what you look at
- what you listen to
- how you dress

What does impurity mean to you?

Look at what Jesus said:

You have heard that it was said, "Do not commit adultery." But I tell you that anyone who looks at a woman lustfully has already committed adultery with her in his heart. (Matthew 5:27–28)

That means your thoughts can be just as sinful as your actions.

• • • • Duh, why didn't I think of that?

God says: "Flee from sexual immorality."

Which means: Run from sexual impurity.

So what God is actually saying is: *Run to purity.*

• • • • plan for purity

- Be wise about what situations you put yourself and your date in.

- Have a plan of escape when tempted.
- Work toward open communication with your date or boyfriend about your desire for purity.
- Date in groups.
- When he drops you off after the date, don't sit for hours parked in the driveway, staring into his eyes—or letting him stare into your chest.

Look at what Amy wrote me about her relationship with her boyfriend, Cody:

> I am crazy about Cody. But I want to honor God in my relationship with him. That's why we have come up with guidelines that we both work to keep to protect us from giving in to tempting moments. We don't go parking alone. We keep our "good nights" brief. No, it's not easy. But it's a lot better than having a baby at my age!

Knowing what God wants for you when it comes to your sex life is a critical step in embracing a lifestyle of purity. Making his desire a reality in your life is where the challenge begins. According to her letter, Amy and her boyfriend both realize they have to do their part to honor God by establishing a plan for purity.

Amy and Cody are off to a good start. The best way to stay away from sin is to plan ahead. Do you have a plan for purity in your own life? If you have a boyfriend, have you talked about working together to stay pure? If you don't have your own guidelines yet, or if you want to add some to your list, keep reading for a few suggestions.

YOU'RE A ONE-MAN WOMAN

Okay, that title sounds like I'm going to tell you not to date three guys at the same time or something, but that's not what I mean. I think you already know cheating on a guy is not a good idea. What I mean is, your purity and your virginity should belong to only one man—the man you marry.

In the Garden of Eden, God said that Adam needed a companion. Not "companions." God didn't send Adam a busload of Dallas Cowboys cheerleaders, a crew of Hooters girls, or a runway full of Victoria's Secret models. He created Adam as a one-woman man. And he created Eve as a one-man woman. He created you in the same way. You haven't been created to be a woman for every man who shows interest in you or even for a few men who say they love you.

A one-man woman realizes:

- She's been created for true love.
- She's been created to share true love with one man in marriage.
- She's been created for only that one man to have the privilege of knowing her, touching her, or being with her physically.

You have to see yourself as a one-man woman, because if you don't think that way from the beginning, it's a lot easier to end up being a two- or three- or four-man woman. Once you make the decision to be a one-man woman, setting boundaries and maintaining those boundaries will be a lot easier.

Jeffrey, I don't wanna sleep with a bunch of guys or anything. But what if I think I've actually found "the one"? I think it might be okay to do some things with him if I love him and really think he's the guy I'll be with forever.

The keyword here is *think*. You may *think* you've met the one man you'll be with forever. But how do you know for sure? Let's say you go ahead and start getting physical with him. Where does it stop? Will you have sex with him if that's what he wants (or if it's what you think you want)? What if you find out one week, one month, or even one year later that the guy you thought was the one…isn't?

When you start doing physical stuff in a relationship, it'll only be a matter of time before you lose sight of what's right and wrong. And once you're so deeply attached to someone, making the right choice in a moment of temptation can be really difficult.

1. Establish boundaries from the beginning.
2. Know your convictions and stick to them.
3. Communicate your convictions.
4. Don't allow him to place you in a tempting environment—*ever*—and resist drawing him into one.
5. Remember: Run to purity!

Infatuation vs. Love

It's hard to know if it's truly love when you think he's as sexy as Keith Urban and has the athletic ability of LeBron James and the talent of

Justin Timberlake. Seriously, knowing the difference between like and love can be incredibly hard. But it's also vital information if you're going to stay a one-man woman, because mistaking infatuation for love can make you do things you'll regret. Fortunately, the Bible offers some help in 1 Corinthians 13. Look at how love is described in these verses.

Love "is patient" (verse 4)

Infatuation isn't. Infatuation is often an uncontrollable, short-lived fascination with someone that ends as quickly as it began. Love is patient and willing to wait and work through tough issues. Infatuation is often ready to give up when things get tough, especially when someone doesn't get their way in the relationship.

Love is "not rude...it is not easily angered" (verse 5)

Love is not a feeling that changes from day to day. When things get tough, love doesn't retaliate, get even, or act in jealousy. Infatuation gets mad, often stays mad, and usually allows emotions to take over and destroy the once feel-good feeling.

Love is "not self-seeking" (verse 5)

This is one area where I see most teens mistake infatuation for love. A guy who loves you should never expect anything but your love in return. Many girls tell me they feel pressured to get physical with their boyfriend to "prove" their love to him or because they feel like they "owe" him something for taking them out. If you feel like you have to prove your loyalty to your boyfriend or have to please him sexually in return for something, then the relationship isn't based on love. Any boy who pressures a girl to please him is seriously self-seeking—he only cares about himself, not you.

Never change your convictions for a guy just because:

- he says, "I love you!"
- he spends a lot of money on you
- you feel like you have to prove your love
- you think it'll make him happy
- you think he'll leave you if you don't

Love "always protects" (verse 7)

Have you ever felt unsafe or seriously uncomfortable on a date? Have you ever had a guy take you to a party where there were drugs, alcohol, or hooking up? If the answer is yes, then you probably aren't in a relationship based upon love. According to 1 Corinthians 13:7, love never places someone in an unsafe environment, no matter the reason or excuse. This should be one of the easiest ways for you to gauge whether or not you're in a relationship founded on love or infatuation. Love will never intentionally place you in a situation where you might get hurt or do something you shouldn't do.

Love "never fails" (verse 8)

Love is a commitment that never fails. It doesn't stop when things go bad. It doesn't end when the relationship gets tough. It doesn't go sour when rumors fly or someone's appearance and weight fluctuate. It doesn't give up or grow tired or bored. Love always remains.

take a break

Is it or isn't it? Here are a few thoughts to help you know if it's really love:

Person or Prize? If you're going out with him because you think it makes you the It Girl, the winner of the hottest guy, or the holder of bragging rights, then it isn't love.

The Grass Looks Greener. If you still find yourself looking for other guys to date, hook up with, or flirt with, then it isn't love.

No Kiss, Just Bliss. If you're in sweetheart bliss just being around him and you don't have to kiss him, touch him, or have any physical contact with him at all, then there's a chance it could be love.

Purse, Coat, and Gloves. If your outfit for a date includes boxing gloves, then it probably isn't love. If you fight or disagree a lot about silly things, or tease, criticize, or make fun of each other to the point of meanness, then there's not much of a future for the two of you.

No Secrets Allowed. Can you talk about what's really important to you? Do you have secret sins you're trying to hide from him? Is there a part of his life he won't let you into? True love is founded on truth. If either of you is pretending the relationship is something it's not, or can't express true feelings, or can't be completely honest, then it ain't love.

No "Ifs." A guy who says, "If you loved me, you would..." doesn't love you. You should not have to do anything to prove your love—especially something you know you shouldn't do.

Guard Your Heart

Above all else, guard your heart,
for it is the wellspring of life.
(Proverbs 4:23)

Guarding your heart is essential to embracing a lifestyle of purity. You may've gone through the last section and figured out exactly what love should look like. But even in a relationship where you really love each other, there's still a chance you could make some big mistakes. And being in love doesn't give you license to do things outside God's will. God never intended for you to give your heart away to more than one person, so you have to be ready to defend it. Sometimes, even kissing a guy can be a dangerous thing. The world tells you a kiss is as innocent and noncommittal as a handshake. But your heart will tell you otherwise.

There are times when simply holding a guy's hand or feeling him close to you will sizzle your heart faster than twelve minutes in a tanning bed. Maybe having a guy touch you in "that way only a guy can" may seem innocent to him. But you know what it can do to you. You have to guard your heart so your emotions won't guide your actions. Because the more you give your heart to a guy, the easier it will become to eventually give him all of you.

So how do you keep your heart safe? When it comes down to it, only you know how to do that, because everyone's different. But here are some suggestions to help you figure it out.

1. Know your edge.

One of the most popular questions girls ask me is "How far is too far?" What they're actually asking is "How far can I go without getting into trouble? How much can I get away with?"

If you were standing on a cliff, would you walk right up to the edge and see how close you could get before you fell? You wouldn't be too smart if you did. A woman who's committed to becoming a woman of God is someone who, rather than asking, "How close to the edge can I get," asks, "How far away from the edge do I need to stay?"

Every girl is wired a little differently in this area.

1. For some, all it takes to approach their edge is having a guy smile at them and tell them they're beautiful.
2. For others, holding hands with a guy places them on their edge.
3. And for many, it can be a kiss or a touch from a guy that puts them on the edge of trouble.

The keyword here is *purity.* Remember, God said to run to purity. You don't need me to draw a chart, list statistics, or walk you through the ABCs of living pure. Only you can determine when the line has been crossed from purity to impurity. You need to know your edge. Know where this point is for you, and then make a commitment to yourself—and to God—never to approach it.

Any girl can buy the lies that Satan sells. You know them. He's probably seduced you with them a time or two before:

- "You love each other. You're not doing anything wrong."
- "It's no big deal. It's only a little further than you went on your last date."
- "It's not sex. It's just oral sex."
- "Come on. Just this one time."
- "It's okay. You've been dating him a long time."

As a woman who wants to be made into God's likeness, you have to take responsibility for pursuing your own personal purity.

2. Know when to take control.

So often girls say things to me like:

- "Things got out of control. I'm not sure how it even happened!"
- "I didn't mean to go this far. One thing just led to another."
- "We didn't start off doing all of this in the beginning. But after dating awhile, it just started to happen."

Here's the deal: *you* are in control. Don't ever let a guy make you feel like you're not. Remember the advice about dating from the last chapter—you have to take control and have conviction. Know where your line is, and when a guy starts to approach it, make sure he doesn't cross it. There are a lot of great guys out there. But don't forget, even the best of guys, in a moment of passion, can quickly lose control. You've gotta be ready to maintain it even when he doesn't.

Imagine if you jumped into a brand-new five-speed Ford Mustang convertible—the ones with the new body style that looks a lot like the classic ones from the sixties—drove onto the interstate, shifted from first to second to third to fourth to fifth gear, and then all of a sudden, at the speed of sixty-plus miles an hour, decided to go from fifth gear to reverse. What do you think would happen?

You'd probably trade your car for an ambulance. Why? Because no matter how sweet that Mustang looks cruising down the interstate, it was never meant to go from fifth to reverse. The same is true with your body. Your body wasn't created to be able to get really physical with a guy and then just "throw it in reverse," draw the line, and stop.

When the physical stuff starts, it's very difficult to stop. There's nothing weird about that—it's how your body's wired. That's why you have to stay really far away from your edge. Because anytime you choose to approach that edge, it'll just be a matter of time before you fall off the cliff.

It's about purity, not virginity. There are a lot of physical acts that don't technically count as sex, but they are just as damaging to you spiritually, physically, and emotionally.

3. Know what you do to him.

By the look on her face I knew she was mad at me before she even said a word. I'd just finished speaking at a teen event in Alabama, and when she approached me, I knew this was going to be an "interesting" exchange of words. The conversation went something like this:

Mad Girl: How do you think I'm dressed?

Me: *(Okay, before I answer this question, you must know there are times when girls ask us guys a question, and no matter how we answer the question, we're going to be in trouble. Let me just say I thought she was dressed very inappropriately. But if I told her that, it could make her even madder. However, if I said she was dressed fine, she would've known I wasn't telling the truth. I really couldn't win. And she knew it. I thought for a moment before answering her.)* How do *you* think you are dressed? *(Ha! This was a good response, wasn't it!)*

Mad Girl: I think this outfit I have on makes me look cute.

Me: Maybe it does make you look cute. But God's not judging you on your fashion sense—and neither are the guys who are looking at you. The question isn't "How good do I look?" It should be "What does how I look say to other people about me?" I'm afraid the answer to the second question wouldn't make you as happy as the answer to the first one.

What *He's* Thinking

For better or worse, guys are really visual people. All they have to do is look at a girl to get excited. That means they notice how you dress. And they decide what kind of girl you are based on how you're dressed. Even if you have no intention of letting a guy touch you, he might get another idea from the cleavage you're showing or the short, short skirt you're wearing. And you might be doing a lot of things in his mind you would *never* do in real life.

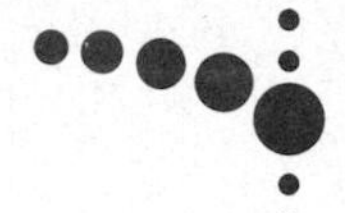

Wait a second. It's not my fault if some guy looks at me and starts to lust. That's his problem, not mine.

Yes and no. Sure, the guy has a responsibility too. But this book isn't for guys—it's for you. So let's focus on your part of the equation. First Corinthians 6:20 says, "Honor God with your body." Your body is not just a place to put cute clothes or a product on display for the guys you walk past in the halls of your school. As a woman trying to live a godly life, you should want to honor God in every area of your life, including how you dress. And wearing things that obviously cause other people to have sinful thoughts is not a way to honor God. Being pure is not just about you. You should try to help others stay pure too.

the Truth

So whether you eat or drink or whatever you do, do it all for the glory of God. Do not cause anyone to stumble.... For I am not seeking my own good but the good of many, so that they may be saved. (1 Corinthians 10:31–33)

4. Know how to say no.

"How can I say no without hurting his feelings?" Lots of teen girls ask me this question. Many of them want to say no to a guy's physical advances, but these girls, who generally aren't shy about anything, are afraid of hurting his feelings. Let me just say, if this guy wants you to do stuff you don't really want to do, you shouldn't care if you hurt his feelings or not. And if he does get angry when you say no, he's definitely not worth worrying about. When it comes to situations like this, I have just seven words for you: *no* is a good word—use it.

I remember quite a few times in high school when I had to take a stand for my convictions by saying no. On one such occasion, it cost me a girlfriend. But once I took a stand for what I knew was right, I became more confident in my own convictions and more ready to take a stand the next time.

Second Timothy 1:7 says, "For God has not given us a spirit of fear and timidity, but of power, love, and self-discipline" (NLT).

5. Know what God says.

There are plenty of reasons not to cross the purity line until you're married. I'll give you four:

- no guilt on your wedding night
- no comparisons to previous bed partners
- no unwanted pregnancy
- no worrying about diseases that leave ugly-looking sores, spots, and warts that appear in very private places

But the ultimate reason you should stay far away from your edge until your wedding night isn't because of consequences, guilt, fear of STDs, or the possibility of an unwanted pregnancy. Sure, all those things are extremely important reasons. However, the number-one reason why you should say no to sex, and all things sex-related, until marriage is *because God said so.*

Freedom

Since God is God, after all, he really doesn't have to have another reason for why you should do what he says. God said it. That's the end of it. But the cool thing is that God does have another reason:

If you choose the purity route until you're married, you'll find *freedom.* And whether you realize it or not, that's what you really want in life. Freedom is what we *all* want in life.

You've heard people say:

"This is *your* life."

"Live it for *you.*"

"Live the way *you* want!"

"Do what *you* want to do!"

Each of these statements has a common thread. Each is ultimately about freedom—freedom to live the way you want, freedom to find the very best in life, freedom to have what'll make you happiest.

The world says:

"Go ahead. Indulge."

"You deserve it."

"He's a hunk."

"It's just one time."

"No one'll get hurt."

"Everyone is doing it."

"No strings attached."

"This is true freedom."

The irony is that the freedom the world claims to give you can only be found in Christ—it's what he promises. Lots of people think if they choose God's way, they're giving up the freedom to live the way they want. The world's way may make you feel free at first, but you'll soon find that it'll make you feel even more imprisoned than you did before. Just think for a second: When you do something wrong, you're weighed down by the fear that you'll get caught. Or you're stuck with some really un-fun consequences, like punishment from your parents, a failing grade, a wrecked car, a pregnancy… The list could go on forever.

And worst of all, pursuing the world's freedom takes you further away from *real* freedom. The freedom found in Christ is built on him—the best, the strongest, the eternal foundation—and it'll never leave you feeling trapped and empty. God's plan isn't about giving up freedom. God's plan is about being free. And Romans 6:16–18 makes it clear that if you choose to follow God's plan, you'll truly be free:

> Offer yourselves to sin, for instance, and it's your last free act. But offer yourselves to the ways of God and the freedom never quits. All your lives you've let sin tell you what to do. But thank God you've started listening to a new master, one whose commands set you free to live openly in *his* freedom! (MSG)

Are you in search of freedom from something?

Regrettable choices?

A failed relationship?

The past?

Guilt?

Sin?

You may think that true freedom can be found in sex. Oral sex. Hooking up. But look again at what God says in Romans. He says if you choose to embrace living this way, this will be "your last free act." The thing the world says will give you true freedom is actually the thing God says will destroy your freedom.

Freedom in God is:

- never relying on a sexual experience to feel fulfilled
- never waking up the next morning with regret
- never experiencing the emotional baggage, pain, or consequences sex outside marriage can bring

It's All About the Future Fun

One teen told me, "Jeffrey, one of the biggest reasons that I'm *not* into God is because he has too many rules I have to follow." That's how a lot of girls think when it comes to sex. They think that if they "follow God's rules," they forfeit the chance to enjoy "all the fun." Again, a lie from the great liar.

Before my daughter Bailey turned two, we bought her a baby pool. (No, I'm not getting off topic. Really. You'll see.) As you can imagine, she loved it. I remember one time she was swimming her little baby bottom off, and I needed to go into the office for a phone call, so I took her out of the pool. She threw one of those fits, something we always said our children would never do. Bailey was pretty upset because, just moments before, she was swimming and having a great time, and now she was being forced to go inside. To put it mildly, she was ticked. In her young mind, she thought I was trying to keep her from having fun. But as you know, I wasn't trying to keep her from having fun; I was trying to protect her. It's crazy to even consider that I would allow Bailey to swim alone. There could've been a huge tragedy waiting if I'd left her in the pool.

The same is true with God when it comes to your sex life. His plan is not designed to keep you from having fun; it's to protect your future fun inside of marriage. When it comes to sex, or any choice you make that's outside his will, he knows there'll be a tragedy waiting if you choose to "swim alone."

God knows what's best for you. He knows what'll keep you safe and secure. A sign of a real woman is understanding that God's ways are best, even when they don't seem very fun right now.

Notice I didn't just say God's ways are good. I said they're *best.* Remember in chapter 5 we talked about letting go of the good in order to get God's best. The same applies to your sex life. It's easy to come up with some "good" reasons to do the stuff you want to do and then use those reasons to justify actions that are outside God's will.

"Good" reasons the world gives for having sex before marriage:

"I'm in love."

"We've planned ahead."

"I'm old enough now."

"It's prom night."

No matter how "good" your reasons are, if you're trying to justify something that's against God's will, you're trading his *best* for the world's *good.* Why would you want to trade down when God is offering you the absolute best there is?

ALERT!

God isn't in the business of just making sure that you have a *good* relationship with the person you happen to be dating this month. God wants you to have the *best.* Sometimes this is difficult to understand. But in order to have the best in your future, there are times when you must be willing to say no to what seems good in the present.

Ultimate Freedom

Look at what one teen wrote to me:

I had sex for the first time in seventh grade and have been sexually active in many relationships since. For a long time I thought that because of my past, I couldn't change and honor God in future relationships. You helped me to see that even though I have done some terrible things, it is never too late to start over.

Remember that cool, little, red drawing board called an Etch A Sketch? I was never very good at creating anything worth a second look. But the great thing about the Etch A Sketch is that when you mess up, no big deal. You shake it up, the screen goes clean, and you can start over again.

the *Truth*

But if we confess our sins to God, he can always be trusted to forgive us and take our sins away. (1 John 1:9, CEV)

It's never too late for you to do the right thing. If you've made bad sexual choices, you can start over. Some call that secondary virginity; others call it getting revirginized. I call it ultimate freedom. Your life is like an Etch A Sketch. And a good shake from God can wipe your screen clean and give you ultimate freedom. But to have it, you need these three things:

1. God

He knows where your edge is. Because he created you, only he holds the blueprints to your existence, and only he is equipped to help you handle this issue. First, if there's anything you regret, ask God to forgive you for the past. As we've discussed repeatedly throughout this book, one of Satan's greatest lies is to convince you that your past will keep you from ever becoming the woman God wants you to be. But look at what the Bible says:

> But if we confess our sins to God, he can always be trusted to forgive us and take our sins away. (1 John 1:9, CEV)

When we ask for forgiveness, he is ready and willing to give it. It could be that your past is the one thing keeping you from truly being made into the woman he desires you to be.

Do you need to walk away from the past? Do you need your screen wiped clean? If so, write a prayer now asking God to clean up the mess of your past.

Once you've asked for forgiveness, you need to work every day to make God the priority in your life. As you do, you'll develop a love for him that'll burn stronger than any other love you might have.

2. The Word

Spending time in God's Word will change the way you think and act. Romans 12:2 says, "Don't be like the people of this world, but let God change the way you think. Then you will know how to do everything that is good and pleasing to him" (CEV). As you commit to spend time getting to know God, he'll equip you with the knowledge of "how to do everything that is good and pleasing to him."

3. You

Remember, you are responsible for yourself. You have to do your part. Establish boundaries in your dating life, commit to pursue purity over impurity, and remember that every day is a new day. The past is the past. You can't change where you've been, but you can control where you go.

My Space

1. Are you living on or over your edge?

2. If yes, what will you commit to do to change that?

3. If no, what will you keep doing to pursue purity rather than impurity?

4. After reading this chapter, what piece of advice will you apply to your life right now?

Chapter 10

Girl Secrets

Some stuff is just too personal to talk about. Or maybe not.

As you might've noticed by now, I'm a pretty big fan of lists. "Here are five things you can do…" "Remember these eight steps…" Blah blah blah. Lists are good for a lot of things. They can help you focus on your goal and all that. But there are some problems that can't be solved with a list. Those kinds of problems are what this chapter is about. So I promise you—no lists in this chapter. Go ahead, do a little dance, breathe a big sigh of relief, cheer, whatever. Enjoy it. This is the only break you get. Ha.

(Also, I'm going to give you a break from the "sarcastic girl" voice. This is one place where a critical voice isn't going to be helpful. So you'll just have to take care of the questioning and arguing yourself for a little bit. I'm not worried. I'm sure you can handle it…ha-ha.)

We all have secrets. We all have things about ourselves we try to hide from others. That's just the way it is. We don't want to be embarrassed or we don't want people to see how vulnerable we are or how much we're hurting. Even us guys have secrets, believe it or not. And we keep them for a lot of the same reasons you do.

I remember having a secret in high school. I was shy and extremely underconfident. I wasn't very athletic. I was skinny, super skinny. I mean turn-me-to-the-side-you-can't-hardly-see-me skinny. And I had so many pimples through most of high school that you could've probably played connect-the-dots on my face. Everybody could see those things, so they were never secrets. But all that stuff was what caused my secret. I would stare into the mirror and hate what I saw, hate myself so much I wanted to die. This was the secret I carried around for years.

I've talked with a lot of girls (and guys) who have secrets—secrets about their past, their bodies, their pain, their families, their addictions, and tons more. Not every person has the same secrets, of course. But since this is a book with a limited number of pages, I'm only going to be able to talk about a few. My experience in counseling has shown me there are some problems that girls have a lot of trouble talking about with anyone. So even if you're not dealing with one of the things I discuss in this chapter, keep reading. Because there's probably someone you know who is.

take a break

Do you have any secrets? If yes, write them here.

Have you talked with someone about them before? Why or why not?

Before you go any farther, I have a request—please, *be honest.* As you read about the secrets of these girls, search your heart and examine how your secrets may be similar to theirs. Consider your life, how you feel about yourself, and what secrets you may have that leave you feeling trapped, guilty, or shameful.

Jamie's Story

"I have a secret," Jamie said as she rolled up the bottom of her pants to show me her leg. "I've been cutting for two years," she said. "It started in junior high. I never felt like I was as good as my older sister. She was like a rock star at our school. Perfect grades, class president, a softball and volleyball athlete. Everyone knew her. Everyone loved her." By now, Jamie was crying uncontrollably as she said, "Who could ever compete with someone so perfect?" Jamie's self-mutilation might've been a secret, but her pain wasn't. The sadness in her eyes gave her away. If anyone was really paying attention, they would've seen how lonely, broken, and insecure she was just by looking at her.

To some people, cutting sounds crazy. Why would anyone want to hurt themselves like that? Well, you may not understand their method, but I bet you understand their motivation. There's a lot of pain inside people like Jamie, and it just keeps building and building until they feel like they can't stand it anymore. Do you know what that feels like?

Why do you cut?

Escape

Release

Curiosity

Attention

To cope

To scream

Though the hurt may seem unbearable, it never justifies the act. And the act will never cure the hurt.

Cutting is just one way desperately sad people can hurt themselves. Holding in your pain and secrets can lead to some dangerous consequences if you let it go that far. I'm not trying to be melodramatic here or anything. Most people who are sad or hurting will be okay eventually. But some won't. I knew one of those people who never got over her pain.

Rebecca's Story

Rebecca was a beautiful girl. Blond hair, popular, from a wealthy family. From the outside looking in, you never would've known how much self-hatred she was hiding.

The first time she made herself throw up was a few weeks before her junior prom. "It was disgusting for me to think about making myself vomit," she told me. "But I convinced myself that the results I saw in the mirror would be worth it." Rebecca read about it online and thought it would be the perfect way to shed a few pounds before the big dance. A few days later and a few pounds lighter, Rebecca was convinced she'd found the perfect way to diet. She was also convinced she had the whole thing under control. She was wrong.

You've probably heard this story before. You most likely had to watch a Lifetime movie about it in health class or something. But this was Rebecca's real life. And it quickly started slipping away from her. Eating and throwing up became routine throughout her senior year of high school. By the time she started college, a skeleton stood in Rebecca's place, someone nothing like the girl she'd been twelve months before. Rebecca's family and friends talked to her again and again about stopping. But she didn't listen. She'd become so concerned with her weight that she was blind to the fact that her addiction to being thin was killing her. She died of a failed kidney just a few months into her sophomore year of college.

Eating disorders are always mentioned when people are talking about "girl problems." But there's a reason for that. You live in a world that puts a lot of pressure on you to be physically flawless. That pressure can lead to anorexia, bulimia, or even overeating (yes, that's an eating disorder too, even though people don't talk about it half as much). Whether or not you've gone as far as starving yourself or gorging yourself, you probably have some understanding of why these girls do this stuff. Maybe you know someone who's throwing up her dinner right this minute.

Rebecca's problem started pretty innocently. She just wanted to be a little thinner for prom. Can you blame her? She wanted to be liked, to be a little closer to perfect. Those feelings seem benign, but you can become obsessed with getting approval from the people around you. You can start feeling like you can't live without it.

Kate's Story

Kate started dating when she was thirteen. She told me she had sex for the first time not long after that. By the time she was sixteen, she had been in a lot of relationships and had sex with lots of people. "I really don't wanna have sex with them," she said to me. "I just want to find the one guy who'll stick around."

What Kate was saying was that she didn't think she could survive without a guy in her life. She quickly became emotionally dependent on the next guy in line. She knew the label many in her school had given her. But she didn't care. She just wanted to feel love from a guy. But in her pursuit of love, all she found was guilt, loneliness, and enough "looking for love in all the wrong places" stories to fill a book.

Are you emotionally dependent on guys?

- Do you feel like there's no way out of a relationship, even when you don't want to be with the guy anymore?

- Are you willing to do whatever you think is necessary to stay in the relationship?
- Are you so concerned about pleasing him that you'll ignore all the things that used to be important to you?
- Do you feel like you need him so much that you'll make excuses for him when he treats you badly?

Critical News!

One in three girls will be in a controlling, or even abusive, relationship before she graduates from high school (from *But I Love Him* by Dr. Jill Murray). And remember, abuse isn't just physical; it can be emotional too. Girls who feel like they absolutely *need* a guy in their lives are much more susceptible to being in these harmful relationships.

Kate didn't like herself enough to believe she deserved something better than jumping from one bad guy to the next. Self-hatred is a symptom of so many of the problems girls—and guys—have. Sometimes it makes you do things you regret. And sometimes it paralyzes you so you can't do anything at all.

Danielle's Story

Danielle was sixteen when it began. She didn't want to get out of bed. Her grades started falling. She just wasn't herself. She knew something was wrong, but when anyone asked, she couldn't say exactly what it was. She was hurting, but she didn't know where. She also didn't know how to stop feeling this way—or even if she really wanted to.

Maybe it was the fact that her parents seemed to always be fighting. Or maybe it was because she continued unsuccessfully to try to lose a few more pounds. It was all those things and none of those things. That's what depression does to you. It causes pain you can't explain—so you don't know how to get rid of it.

Critical News!

- 1 in 8 teens is affected by depression.
- Teen depression is more common in females than males.
- 3 to 5 percent of teens are affected by depression each year. (National Center for Health and Wellness, 2006)

Did you see yourself in Jamie, Rebecca, Kate, or Danielle? Maybe just a little? If you did, does it offer a bit of hope to know you're not alone?

I could spend all day telling you these stories, explaining to you why this girl stays with a boyfriend who hits her or that girl won't eat even though she only weighs eighty pounds. But that doesn't mean I completely understand any of it. And it definitely doesn't mean I know exactly how to fix it. But even though I don't, I know God does. I know he understands.

Yes, I know what you're thinking. It seems really trite to bring it back around to God. But I've never been that cool in the first place. And here I'm just giving up. If it's trite, then I'll have to be trite. Because it's true. Whether your secret is one I've talked about or one I haven't ever heard of, God knows exactly what's going on in your heart and in your life. Just look at what the Bible says:

> Praise be to the Lord, to God our Savior,
> who daily bears our burdens. (Psalm 68:19)

And then, look at this:

> Come to me, all you who are weary and burdened, and I will give you rest. (Matthew 11:28)

Remember, one of the foundational truths of this book is that if God says it, he means it. When the psalm says he bears our burdens, it doesn't just mean he knows about them. It means he actually picks them up and carries them for us. This is good stuff to know when you feel so dragged down by your secrets that you can't go another step.

This is usually the point where I'd whip out the 1-2-3-step solution to your struggle. But I already promised you that's not going to happen. Unlike those over-the-counter zit zappers that work overnight (yeah, right), it's impossible to give you a quick fix. You know your problem didn't just appear in a day. And it won't be solved in twenty-four hours either. Yeah, this sounds pretty discouraging. Why am I even writing this chapter if I can't help you, right? Well, I said I couldn't *fix* anything. But what I can do is try to point you in the right direction so, over time, you'll find your way to the solution.

WARNING!

The following suggestions may closely resemble a list or a series of steps, but do not be deceived. If they're not numbered, it's not a list. And if they're not leading you to a specific goal, then they're not steps. So technically I've kept my promise. I said no lists and I meant it. (Sort of...)

One thing you have to do to get going in the right direction is...

Be Honest with Yourself

Remember back at the beginning of this chapter when I told you I only had one request? I asked you to be honest—honest with yourself. Sometimes the hardest part of overcoming a problem isn't admitting it to someone else; it's admitting it to yourself. What do I mean by that? Well, of course you already know about the problem—you're the one who has it, after all. But just because you know it's there doesn't mean you're willing to admit that it's hurting you. You probably make excuses for what you're doing, convince yourself it isn't that bad, tell yourself you can handle it on your own.

As long as you deny how much your secret is dragging you down, you'll never be able to get out from under it. Sometimes you need someone else to help you be really honest. That's when it's...

Time to Talk

You have to know you were never meant to face your struggles alone. And this is exactly why God has given you people in your life who care for you.

A lot of girls won't tell anyone about what's going on because they're afraid of what other people will think of them. Yeah, there are people out there who might make fun of you or not take you seriously or think you're crazy. But there are a lot more people who will listen to you and help you feel better.

And remember, if you feel like there's no one you can talk to, you can always talk to God. When you do that, you're not just talking to thin air. Believe me, he's listening.

the *Truth*

You hear, O LORD, the desire of the afflicted; you encourage them, and you listen to their cry. (Psalm 10:17)

take a break

Is there someone in your life you can talk with about your secret?

If yes, write their name here.

Write a commitment to yourself that you'll go and talk with someone about what's hurting you.

The biggest obstacle you face in daring to talk to someone and beginning to deal with your problem is believing things that just aren't true. So, please…

Don't Buy the Lies

Satan wants you to believe your secret is something you should feel ashamed of. He wants you to think you should never talk to anyone. He wants to convince you that no one will understand if you tell them. He'll get you thinking crazy things, like that you'd be better off if you just didn't tell anyone.

The lies:

You'll hurt them.
You'll make them mad.
They'll be crushed.
They won't understand.
They'll kick you out.

Don't buy it. You're not messed up, weird, dysfunctional, or a freak. I'll tell you a million times until you hear it—we all have secrets, every one of us. The difference between those who overcome their problems and those who stay trapped by them is belief—belief that God's truth is stronger than Satan's lies.

And even if you still refuse to tell a soul about how much you're hurting, you have to know…

You Can't Keep Secrets from God

Your secret is no secret to God. Psalm 44:21 says, "He knows the secrets of the heart." Your story is no surprise to him. I've said this before, but it's worth saying again: God sees you as you are right now, and he loves you. It may be hard to believe right this minute, but he made you for a special purpose. And he wants to restore you to the woman he made you to be.

Alert!

No matter what has gone on in your past,
No matter how trapped you feel,
No matter how lonely it seems,
No matter how sharp the pain,
No matter how deep the cut,
No matter how hidden the secret,
You are okay with God.

the Truth

And the God of all grace, who called you to his eternal glory in Christ, after you have suffered a little while, will himself restore you and make you strong, firm and steadfast. (1 Peter 5:10)

So if you're even starting to believe me just a little bit, you've got to hear me when I say…

Hope Is Yours for the Taking

You may hate your life right now—or at least not enjoy it too much. And you might feel about ready to give up. That seems like the easiest solution, right? But believe it or not, it's the worst possible thing you could do. Because if you can just have a little hope, just try to believe that God can help you through this, you'll find something better than you ever thought you could have.

the *Truth*

Hope does not disappoint us, because God has poured out his love into our hearts by the Holy Spirit, whom he has given us. (Romans 5:5)

I told you at the beginning of this book that what I have for you in these pages won't always be easy. This definitely isn't easy. But it's worth every step of it. Hope is yours for the taking, but you've got to actually step out and take it. And that means trusting God, and trusting he'll send help for you.

I patiently waited, LORD, for you to hear my prayer.
You listened and pulled me from a lonely pit
full of mud and mire.

You let me stand on a rock with my feet firm,
and you gave me a new song,
 a song of praise to you.
Many will see this, and they will honor
 and trust you, the LORD God.
You bless all of those who trust you. (Psalm 40:1–4, CEV)

I know you're practically swimming in Scripture now, after all the verses I've thrown at you. But slow down and read that last one again—out loud. Imagine how much hope the psalmist must have been filled with when he wrote that. Then write down this verse and keep it with you. Hang it in your locker or on the mirror in your bedroom or bathroom. Keep a copy of it in your purse. Read it again and again. And as you honestly face your secret, begin to talk with others about it, commit not to buy Satan's lies, and know that God understands where you are, you'll see that he's picking you up and carrying you through all of it. God can use even the darkest times in your life to complete his plan for you. Nothing is so bad that he can't make it into something good.

My Space

What steps will you take now to find freedom from your secret?

Chapter 11

Go to Hell

The problem with saying nothing is what your silence says.

Locker 121. I still remember my junior-high locker number all these years later. As much time as I spent inside it, there's really no way I could forget. It's not as bad as you'd imagine—being in a locker, I mean—especially if it's before lunch and you're stuck in there with a PB & J sandwich and a Dew.

I didn't go in my locker of my own free will. I was forced in by several punks in my school. And the ringleader of the punkheads was a guy named Eric. Eric and I were enemies. He used to sit behind me in algebra class and thump me on the back of the head. And to this day, if someone pops me upside the head, it quickly brings back memories of 9:00 a.m. algebra, Eric, and headaches.

I often wondered why Eric didn't like me. That is, until the day he told me it was because I was a Christian. All through junior high and high school, it seemed Eric's goal in life, other than acting like a complete "donkey," was to totally ruin six years of my existence.

Therefore, you can imagine, when I heard God tell me that he wanted me to talk to Eric about what it meant to be a Christian, I assumed God was mistaken. I remember laughing at first. But he wasn't joking. God really wanted me to talk about him with Eric.

I intentionally ignored his request for four months. And I was miserable because of it. I knew what God wanted me to do. And I knew I would stay miserable until I did it. So finally I called Eric on the phone, in part because I really enjoyed my nose and didn't want to lose it if Eric decided to take a swing at me. Having prepared my thoughts long before I made the call, I must say, I gave the speech of my life. And to my surprise, Eric listened. Giving myself a big high-five for a job well done, I then finished by asking if Eric would like to pray to receive Jesus into his life. Eric politely said no. And he hung up the phone.

What? You have got to be kidding, I thought. It wasn't supposed to work this way. I remember praying to God and saying, *I did what you asked me to, and you didn't come through for me! I put my neck on the line with a guy I can't even stand to look at, and it didn't work!* I was mad. Mad at God.

take a break

Is there someone in your life who doesn't have a personal relationship with Jesus? Write their name(s) here.

It took me a while, but I learned a lot about my witness through this experience. I learned that as a person being made into the likeness of God, there's much more to sharing my faith than the outcome. I learned that my witness is an integral part of who I am as a Christian. And every day, regardless of how others respond, I have a responsibility to live out a life of witness.

The Life You Live > The Words You Say

What if you walked into school this week to find every student and teacher seated in the gymnasium? And what if the principal called you to join him at center court? And then, what if, one by one, every student and teacher in your school walked across the court, grabbed the microphone, and were each given thirty seconds to proclaim to everyone how you've witnessed to them with the way you live your life. What would they say? What would you *want* them to say?

Actions speak louder than words. And people *are* watching. My life is on display for everyone I come in contact with. My family, my close friends, my co-workers, and my neighbors, the person who scans my groceries at Kroger, the waiter who brings me my plate of catfish and pitcher of iced tea at my favorite Nashville restaurant, the people I sit next to on a plane every time I travel, my daughter's soccer coach—every day my life impacts the lives of others. And with each encounter, I have the opportunity—the responsibility—to show them there's something different about me because I'm a follower of Jesus. And often this happens without ever opening my mouth.

The same is true for you. Every day, in every relationship, with every encounter, you have the chance to be Jesus to your world. Most of the time you don't do it with what you say but with what you do. And for a lot of the people you cross paths with, this could be the only glimpse of God they ever get.

• • • • question

Does the life your non-Christian friends see you live *with* Jesus differ from the lives they live *without* him?

Forget the Fear Factor

Reality TV has proven over and over that people will do crazy things that test their endurance, their faith, and their fears just to get their fifteen minutes of fame.

take a break

Would you:

- eat a pizza covered in tomato sauce, cheese, and leeches?
- sing really, really badly and be made fun of by judges on national television?
- drink an ice cream smoothie with bananas, strawberries, and calf brains?

It's amazing how so many people are willing to set aside their fears in pursuit of things that will bring them temporary satisfaction. Imagine what could happen in your life and the lives of those in your world if you set aside your fears, not just to have a moment on TV and a big cash prize, but to see someone's life changed forever.

It took me four months of ignoring what God asked me to do before I finally chose to share my faith with Eric. Why? Because I was afraid of what Eric might think about me. I was afraid of what Eric might say to me. I was afraid of what Eric might *do* to me…like give me another closeup look at the inside of locker 121.

This is exactly how Satan works. He wants to scare you and me into believing that when we speak to others about God, we'll be ridiculed or picked on. Yes, each of these outcomes is a possibility. But when you choose to let God make you into the woman he desires, look at what the Bible says will happen:

God's Spirit doesn't make cowards out of us.
(2 Timothy 1:7, CEV)

As you allow God to work in your life, he'll replace:

your cowardice with courage
your fear with faith
your hesitation with hope
your panic with power
your worry with wonder

When God Asks, He Provides

As you commit to God's plan for your life, get ready. Because along with this commitment comes responsibility—the responsibility to share God with others. When you start embracing your true role as a woman of God by fully submitting your life to him, God will call you to do great things for him. There's no greater privilege in life than sharing the saving message of Jesus with someone else. Sometimes talking to a person about Jesus may seem impossible. But make no mistake, when God calls you to do something:

He'll *never* require something of you that's impossible.

He'll *never* require something of you that you have to face alone.

First Corinthians 1:25 says, "Even when God is weak, he is

stronger than everyone else" (CEV). Even in God's weakness (of which he has none, by the way), he's still stronger than the greatest human strength. When talking with someone about Jesus, remember, you're not alone. When God asks, he provides:

- the way
- the words
- the courage
- the outcome

the *Truth*

Jesus looked at them and said, "With man this is impossible, but with God all things are possible." (Matthew 19:26)

A Command, Not a Question

In his final moments on earth before his ascension, Jesus could've chosen any number of directives for us. He chose just one. Check it out:

> Jesus, undeterred, went right ahead and gave his charge: "God authorized and commanded me to commission you: Go out and train everyone you meet, far and near, in this way of life, marking them by baptism in the threefold name: Father, Son, and Holy Spirit. Then instruct them in the practice of all I have commanded you. I'll be with you as you do this, day after day after day, right up to the end of the age." (Matthew 28:18–20, MSG)

Obviously, Jesus thought evangelism was a high priority. Standing atop that mountain, having a conversation with the disciples, Jesus gave a powerful command to those men—and ultimately to each of us. It was a command to *go.*

I know you might be thinking, *Well, I really don't like to be told what to do.* I understand that. I don't always either. But rather than look at it as a command, consider this: you've been given the privilege of sharing the most important, life-changing news with those in your world. That's really not a command. That's a gift. And if you don't talk with your friends about Jesus, who will?

It's Not About You

Remember how I said I was mad at God when he told me to witness to my biggest enemy, who then turned me down when I asked him to accept Jesus? Do you think my feelings were justified? I was mad because things didn't work out the way I wanted them to. But here's the problem—I believed it was *my* responsibility to save Eric. I was carrying the burden, assuming that it was up to me to change Eric's life. And since this didn't happen in the one phone call with him, I thought I'd failed. And when I felt inadequate, I looked for someone to blame. And I blamed God.

In the months that followed, God started to show me it wasn't my responsibility to change Eric, or anyone else for that matter. Because I can't. Only God can do that. God helped me understand that he didn't tell me to go *save* Eric. He just told me to *go.*

•••• hit pause

If you know someone in your life who's not a believer and you haven't talked with them about it, what's keeping you from doing it now?

If you knew that every time you talked to someone about Jesus they would accept him as their personal Savior, would you tell more people about him?

I'm pretty confident your answer would be yes. Why is that? Because you wouldn't have to be afraid of failing or looking stupid. God helped me understand that choosing to talk with someone about him isn't about success or failure. You need to know that if God has laid it on your heart to share his message with someone, then he already has it worked out. Regardless of the immediate outcome, obedience is all that's required of you. You can't control someone's response. All you can control is your obedience.

•••• Conversation Starters

- Do you believe there is a God?
- I'd like to tell you how I started a personal relationship with God.
- We're having a youth event at our church. Would you like to come?
- We've been friends for a while, and I've never talked to you about the most important thing in my life. Can I tell you now?
- How do you think someone becomes a Christian?

- What do you think it takes to get into heaven?
- If you were to die tonight, where would you spend eternity?

Understand the Mission

I know someone who's in hell today. At least I think he is. I met this man when I was in college. He told me he didn't believe in God, and he didn't want a relationship with him. He was an alcoholic, and several years later he died a miserable death from a failed liver.

Do you know someone who's not a believer? Have you talked with them about Jesus? Let me be brutally honest for a minute. What I'm about to say won't be easy to read, but this is the real deal: if you know someone who's not a believer, and you choose not to share the saving message of Jesus with them, then it's as if you're saying to them, "Go to hell!"

I know you're probably thinking, *That's pretty harsh, Jeffrey.* You're right. It is harsh. It's also true. If we don't care enough about the people in our lives to share Jesus with them, then we don't care enough to see that they spend eternity with God in heaven. Simply put, we don't care for them enough to try to keep them out of hell.

As you begin to see your interactions with people as opportunities to save them from hell, you'll start to grasp the urgency before you, as a woman on a mission to help change the world. You don't have to stand on a stage to be used in this way. You don't have to write a book, be an American Idol, or do stupid stuff on MTV like Johnny Knoxville in order to have a voice. You just have to understand your mission as a follower of Jesus. This mission isn't about your personal success, popularity, or wealth. It's about your willingness to be used by God to help people step from death to life. It's about saying, "I will go."

> **the *Truth***
>
> **It's urgent that you listen carefully to this: Anyone here who believes what I am saying right now and aligns himself with the Father...has at this very moment the real, lasting life and is no longer condemned to be an outsider. This person has taken a giant step from the world of the dead to the world of the living.**
>
> **(John 5:24, MSG)**

Know Your Story

There will be many memorable moments in the story of your life. Your first date. Your first kiss. Your first zit. But the greatest moment of the story is the moment you stepped from death to life, from sinner to forgiven, from condemned to transformed. Not only did this moment change you, it can also be a story used to change others, if you'll let it.

The Bible tells us, "Always be prepared to give an answer to everyone who asks you to give the reason for the hope that you have" (1 Peter 3:15).

Sharing the message of salvation with others isn't rocket science. It's just about being real, being genuine, and being you. You have an incredible story to tell. You have to realize this is true. And you also have to realize you could be the only light in a friend's life.

Jeffrey, give me a break. I don't know enough about the Bible to witness to anyone. I'll just screw it up because there's too much I don't know.

I hear you. But there will always be things we don't know. I've been doing this ministry stuff for a long time, and there are still things about the Bible I don't know. Besides, it isn't about having full knowledge of Scripture. It's about sharing what you do know. And what you do know is what God has done *for you* in your own life. Of course, the more Scripture you know, the better prepared you are. John 3:16 is a great verse. So are Romans 10:9 and Romans 10:13. Plus, you'll also find some help in answering a few of the really big questions in the next section of this chapter. But if someone asks you a question you just don't know the answer to, be honest about your lack of knowledge. Tell your friend that you'll find an answer for them. And then stick to your word. Go talk with a parent or pastor, or go to www.jeffreydean.com and e-mail me. Get an answer to your friend's question, and then go back and share it with them.

Get Your Game Face On

The more you let God change you, the more people will notice a change in you, especially your unsaved friends. They'll see God's character in you. They may notice how you treat others or that you pray before eating lunch at school. Be ready. God will use these moments to bring people to you to share his truth with them. Today you'll most likely come in contact with someone who's not a Christian. Will you be ready?

When you're witnessing, you have to expect some tough questions. Nonbelievers will see you as a representative of Christianity, and they may want you to explain your stance on some of the controversial topics Christians are involved in. You need to be prepared for questions like these. Remember, you don't have to have all the answers to everything (and if you don't know the answer, don't just make something up), but knowing what God's Word says about a few of the big ones will help you be a more effective witness.

Question 1: Is homosexuality wrong?

This is a tough one. It's not so much that the answer is hard to find—there's scripture that states clearly that it's wrong:

> God let them follow their own evil desires. Women no longer wanted to have sex in a natural way, and they did things with each other that were not natural. Men behaved in the same way. They stopped wanting to have sex with women and had strong desires for sex with other men. They did shameful things with each other, and what has happened to them is punishment for their foolish deeds. (Romans 1:26–27, CEV)

It's tough because homosexuality is more accepted in our society now, and saying that it's wrong can make you seem intolerant. And if people think you're intolerant, they're less likely to listen to what you have to say. But you also can't ignore what God's Word says. There's no easy way to handle this. You'll meet people who believe that homosexuals are born with same-sex attraction and that they didn't choose to be gay. You have to know that God didn't create anyone to be homosexual. It's a sin, and it's not part of God's plan. Saying that to someone, however, is not as easy as me writing it in this book.

The best thing to do is remember that you're not anyone's judge. Only God can do that. This will help you be more humble when you share parts of God's Word that aren't so welcome to some people. All you can do when you're faced with issues like homosexuality is let people know what the Bible says—and also let them know that you love them. It may seem impossible to do both at the same time, but God's got a knack for making the impossible possible. All you have to do is ask for his help.

If you know someone who's struggling with homosexuality (it might even be you), and they're not sure what to do about those feelings, you need to let them know they're not alone. Be someone they can talk to. Then tell them they should also talk...

With God: Let them know that God loves them completely. Their struggle is no surprise to him, and he wants to help them break free of it. They should talk to him and ask for strength and guidance.

With Someone Who Will Help: Help them find someone they can trust who will be both honest and kind. Maybe your pastor or youth director or a parent or teacher you know well.

It's important to know that giving in to homosexuality is no more or less wrong than cheating on a test or running a red light. Sin is sin, no matter what sin it is. And God is big enough to handle it and help anyone through it.

Question 2: Are all religions the same?

Not all religions are the same. Some worship false gods. Some believe in God but don't believe that Jesus is his Son. Some believe Jesus was a real person but don't accept the fact that he died for us on the cross and was resurrected from the dead. Some religions don't believe the Bible is the infallible Word of God.

Christianity accepts God as the only God and believes that Jesus is the Son of God, who came to earth, died for humankind, and conquered death by coming back to life and proving that he is the one true Savior of the world. We believe the Bible is God's Word and the ultimate authority for everything we do. To be a Christian means "one is a follower of Christ."

Christianity is based on a person's willingness to believe in and choose to live for Jesus. Christians believe that faith in Jesus is the only way to get to heaven. You can't just be a "good person" or just do "good deeds" (though if you believe in Jesus, you will want to do those things, of course). There's only one path to eternal life, and it's through Jesus. John 14:6 says, "Jesus answered, 'I am the way and the truth and the life. No one comes to the Father except through me.' "

Question 3: Why does God let bad things happen to good people?

"Life's not fair," Jared said in a recent letter to me. "My dad is gone, my mom is depressed, school sucks, and I'm sick of it. I try to do what is right, but nothing seems to go my way!" Can you relate? I know I can. There've been many times in my life when I've had questions about why life can be so unfair. You'll probably ask this a lot too. And you'll most likely have other people ask you this question when they find out you're a Christian.

God has given us a great gift—a gift that people misuse all the time. He's given you and me the free will to live as we please. And because we have the ability to choose, we can often choose the wrong things. So why did God give us the freedom of choice if he knew we could abuse it? God didn't create clones (and aren't you glad he didn't?). He loves us and wants us to love him in return. However, true love can't be forced or manipulated. So since God wanted real love from us, he had to give us the ability to choose. So we can choose to love him…or not love him. And that means we have the freedom to choose to do wrong. Because there's wrong in the world, many bad things happen to people who don't deserve them.

Second (this isn't the easy part to hear), there will be times in life when you have questions you may never have answers for. We'll never fully understand why God does all that he does and allows all that he allows until we reach heaven. The Bible says:

> For who among men knows the thoughts of a man except
> the man's spirit within him? In the same way no one
> knows the thoughts of God except the Spirit of God.
> (1 Corinthians 2:11)

> As you do not know the path of the wind,
>   or how the body is formed in a mother's womb,
> so you cannot understand the work of God,
>   the Maker of all things. (Ecclesiastes 11:5)

Maybe your mom or dad has left your family or you've lost a loved one or you've been mistreated, abused, or abandoned by someone close to you. When you can't find a good reason for why such things happen, remember that God fully understands your pain. He suffered the greatest injustice of all time: allowing his perfect Son, Jesus, to be arrested, beaten, whipped, spit on, cursed at, and then nailed to a cross to die. He never deserved such treatment. But he did it for you—for all of us.

Remember, whether you're in your rock-star moment or kissing the asphalt of life, God is always on your side. Even when answers to life's troubles are hard (or even impossible) to find, God says, "I will always be with you and help you" (Joshua 1:5, CEV).

Don't Give Up

Talking with Eric about Jesus didn't produce the results I wanted overnight. But God used my willingness to tell Eric my story as a first step in Eric's journey. Sometimes one conversation is all it takes to bring a friend to Jesus. Other times, a lifetime of prayer and patience will be needed. Just as God has never given up on you, don't you give up on anyone.

• • • •pray it

If you're serious about reaching those in your world with the message of Jesus, God will take your request very seriously. Pray that:

- God will give you the opportunity
- God will give you the boldness
- God will give you the words

Everyone you know has one thing in common: they all will go to either heaven or hell. Let God use you to bring those in your life to him. There truly is no greater privilege. Believe me, I know. A year after graduation, Eric found me and told me he had found Jesus. He thanked me for not giving up on him.

How to Talk to a Friend About Jesus

1. Start with your story:

- Who God is to you
- What you believe about God
- What God did for you
- How God changed you

2. Ask questions like:

- Do you believe in God?
- What do you believe about God?
- What confuses you the most about God?

3. Ask the most important question:

- Do you know what it means to ask God into your life? Do you want to ask him to be in your life now?

4. Share the following verses:

- "God loved the people of this world so much that he gave his only Son, so that everyone who has faith in him will have eternal life and never really die." (John 3:16, CEV)

  the point: God loved you enough to let his Son die for you. Even though you're not perfect, he sacrificed his Son in your place so you could still spend eternity with him.

- "All of us have sinned and fallen short of God's glory." (Romans 3:23, CEV)

  the point: We're all sinners. Which means all of us need God's help to get into heaven.

- "Sin pays off with death. But God's gift is eternal life given by Jesus Christ our Lord." (Romans 6:23, CEV)

  the point: Since we're all sinners, we don't deserve to go to heaven. But Jesus died in our place and came back to life. He now offers us a gift of eternal life rather than death.

- "But God showed how much he loved us by having Christ die for us, even though we were sinful." (Romans 5:8, CEV)

  the point: You are so loved by God that he let his Son die in your place, so that you wouldn't have to spend eternity in hell separated from God.

- "So you will be saved, if you honestly say, 'Jesus is Lord,' and if you believe with all your heart that God raised him from death. God will accept you and save you, if you truly believe this and tell it to others." (Romans 10:9–10, CEV)

  the point: If you believe that Jesus died for you and came back to life, and you ask him to save you, he will.

My *S*pace

The more you choose to talk with others about Jesus, the easier it'll become. If there's someone in your life who you know needs him, what will you do about it?

Write a prayer asking God to give you the courage to talk with others about him.

Write the names of these people as a reminder to pray for them and commit to talk to them about God.

1.

2.

3.

4.

5.

Chapter 12

What's the Purpose?

Life gets confusing, but you don't need to stay lost. (God knows the way.)

Dear Jeffrey,

I am seventeen and graduating from high school this year. I have already decided on which college I will attend, but have not declared a major. I haven't been sexually active, partied, or made any huge choices I now regret. I guess you could say that I have done pretty much what I am supposed to do up to this point. But what is bothering me is that I don't feel like I have a purpose in life right now. I have been praying all the time, asking God to show me what he wants for my life but have not received a clear direction from him on my future. I want to do his will, but I can't say that I really know what his will is. How am I supposed to live for God when I am not sure what it is that I have been created to live for? Any advice you can offer me would be great.

Thanks,

Heath

Heath has a problem I think all of us have at some point. This is one that crosses the gender divide. He wants to feel like he has a purpose. Like what he's doing is leading him toward an important goal. Like what he's doing matters.

Clearly understanding your purpose in life, and then knowing how to live out that purpose, isn't always easy. But know this: God doesn't want to keep you in the dark about what you were made to do. His timing may be different from yours, but he wants to reveal more of himself to you daily. And as you grow in him, God's plan for your life will become clearer.

Heath asked me three questions in his letter:

1. Do I have a purpose?
2. How do I know what my purpose is?
3. How do I live out my purpose?

There's nothing wrong with asking these questions—and maybe not getting all the answers right away. What's important is how you choose to handle the search for your purpose. Hopefully my answers to these three questions will help you.

Question 1: Do I Have a Purpose?

We've already discussed this question a little bit in chapter 5. When I explained to you how to obey God, I said that an important part of obedience is believing he has a purpose for you. Do you believe that now? Or are you still not sure?

Some people have to wait much longer than they'd like to find out what their purpose is. And while you're waiting, you can start doubting. If you're still questioning whether God really has a plan for your life, read these verses:

> For everything, absolutely everything, above and below, visible and invisible,... *everything* got started in him and finds its purpose in him. (Colossians 1:16, MSG)

> But with your own eyes
> you saw my body being formed.
> Even before I was born,
> you had written in your book
> everything I would do. (Psalm 139:16, CEV)

> The LORD will fulfill his purpose for me.
> (Psalm 138:8)

You are no accident. Psalm 138:8 proclaims that God will fulfill his purpose for you. You do have a purpose. It's a God-given purpose. And God wants to help you fulfill it. But while you're waiting for your "big" purpose, you also have a purpose that's constant, from the moment you accept Christ until the day you go to live with him in heaven—witnessing to others. I've said it again and again: your greatest privilege—and your greatest responsibility—is to be God's mirror in your world. This is a purpose you don't have to wait for God to reveal to you.

the *Truth*

**Everything was created through him;
nothing—not one thing!—
came into being without him.
What came into existence was Life,
and the Life was Light to live by.
The Life-Light blazed out of the darkness;
the darkness couldn't put it out.
(John 1:3–5, MSG)**

God planned all of creation before time on earth began. Before there was light, animals, food, mountains, oceans, or deserts, God had it all planned out in his heart. When he dreamed the idea of creation, you were a part of that dream. He dreamed *you.* So no matter how insecure you feel, no matter how unworthy you feel, no matter how afraid you feel, you can't let that stop you from pursuing God's purpose for you.

When you're asking and he's not answering, you have to trust that he will answer some day. And until then, you have to do all you can for him. You can't sit back and think, *When I lose twenty pounds, then I'll feel better about myself and I'll be able to talk to people about God.* Or *I don't know enough about the Bible yet to do anything for God. Once I know more, then I'll do what he wants.* You're who he made you to be *right now,* and he has things for you to do *right now.* Don't let anything hold you back.

Question 2: How Do I Know What My Purpose Is?

Wouldn't it be great if every day you received an e-mail from God with specific instructions? How cool would it be if God gave you a road map each day detailing what you should do, where you should go, who you should talk to, and what you should avoid? It seems like life would be much more manageable that way, doesn't it? Never having to question, think, or make tough decisions. Never second-guessing your choices or wondering, *What if?*

What would happen if today God decided to reveal to you every detail about the rest of your life?

- who you'll marry
- what your occupation will be
- the names of your children and what they'll look like
- how those closest to you will die and when
- exactly when, where, and how you'll die

At first, it may seem cool to have an inside scoop on the rest of your life. However, after a while, living that way would also be pretty boring. Life would become nothing more to you than a checklist of events. There would be no wonder, no adventure, no anticipation, and no quest. You'd simply clock in, perform your duties, and then clock out. You'd never be driven to figure anything out or search for the answer or prayerfully seek God's guidance to find the right way to go. Life would be routine and meaningless.

There's a word that perfectly describes the kind of person you'd become: *robot.*

God could choose today to give you the blueprints for the rest of your life. And there are times when that offer might seem very tempting. However, when God created you, he didn't create a robot. Instead, he created a *woman* who thinks for herself. And remember, being made into the woman he desires isn't always easy. And finding your purpose isn't either. But when you do find it, you'll celebrate so much more because you worked to get there instead of just letting God hand you the solution. Until then, though, it'll take time.

Time in the Word

It's impossible to consistently know and do God's will if you don't spend time with him. The Bible is a guide for our lives that God has given us.

Look at Psalm 119:104–105:

I gain understanding from your precepts....
Your word is a lamp to my feet
and a light for my path.

Psalm 119 makes it clear that by spending time in the Word, you'll gain understanding. As you commit to spend time in the Word, you'll develop a greater understanding of who God is. As you begin to know him more, he'll reveal to you a greater understanding of his plan and purpose for your life.

• • • • The 1:1:1 Plan

One Passage of Scripture + Once a Day + One Week =
Finding Your Purpose

Repetition is key. There are times when I read the Bible and then forget what I read as soon as I walk away. Going back and reading the same verse over will help you absorb the truth of Scripture. And, as Psalm 119:9 says, this is the way to live a life that honors God:

> How can a young person live a clean life?
> By carefully reading the map of your Word.
> (Psalm 119:9, MSG)

Creative ways to spend time in the Word:

1. Grab your Bible and journal, and find your favorite quiet spot—a park, your backyard, or the lake.
2. Go to Starbucks for some Bible and bean time.
3. Get a few friends together for a sleepover, and instead of watching a movie or talking about guys, start a conversation about a scripture you've been reading and encourage one another to spend more time in the Word.
4. Start a Bible club at your school. Commit to meet once a week to dive into the Word and pray together.

Time in Prayer

Write down the answers to the following questions about your closest friend:

- What's their favorite color?
- Who's their favorite musician or band?
- What's their MySpace address?
- How many times have they been to the principal's office?

Have you ever stopped to wonder why you know so much about the people in your life who are important to you? The reason is, you've made it a priority to spend time with those people. In short, time = knowledge.

The same is true when it comes to your relationship with God. You'll know him better as you spend time talking with him. When you do, he'll reveal himself to you in ways he never has before. And the more time you invest in your relationship with God, the more important your relationship with him will become to you.

Look at what Mark 11:24 says:

> That's why I urge you to pray for absolutely everything, ranging from small to large. Include everything as you embrace this God-life, and you'll get God's everything. (MSG)

Mark 11:24 says it all: embrace a life of prayer with God, and God will give you everything.

• • • • • Have an Awesome Prayer Life

1. Escape

   Prayer can happen anytime, anywhere. But choosing a specific place to escape to, away from distractions, can help you focus on God and not on the busyness of your life.

2. Schedule

   Strive to develop a habit of praying at the same time each day. Log it on your PDA, phone, or laptop, and treat prayer just like a daily meeting. If you're not a morning person, don't sweat it. Make your prayer time an afternoon thing after school or in the evening before bed. There's no right or wrong way to do it. Find out what works for you and stick to it.

3. Shuffle
   Shuffle your prayer experience. One day pray for yourself, the next pray for someone at school, then a family member, then a friend—you get the point.
4. Journal
   Keeping a prayer journal is a great way to keep your prayer life organized. This'll remind you of specific things you want to pray for and help you see how God answers so many of your prayers.
5. Talk
   Talk to God like you would talk to your best friend over coffee.

Time Listening to God

Consider all the things you listen to:

- music
- friends
- MTV
- your dog (questionable…)
- parents

Now consider how much time to you spend listening to God. As we discussed in chapter 5, God wants to talk to you. Proverbs 1:5 says, "Let the wise listen and add to their learning, and let the discerning get guidance." Choosing to listen to God will help you gain an understanding of the purpose he's created you for.

give it a shot

One teen told me his drive time to school is typically the time when he pops in his favorite CD. In an effort to spend more time talking and listening to God, he made a commitment to spend the first half of the twenty-minute drive listening to music and the second half praying and listening to God. He explained that applying this to his morning commute has been a positive way to start living a God-focused day. Find a little window in your life to give over to God. Just a small amount of time spent with him will make a big difference.

Time Waiting

We live in an instant-message, ATM, DSL, drive-through, got-to-have-it-now world. Waiting isn't always fun. And sometimes it really stinks. But God says sometimes waiting is a necessary part of realizing our true purpose in life.

Moses waited 40 years before fulfilling his purpose to help lead the Israelites out of captivity. Noah built an ark and waited 120 years before it ever floated. David waited many sleepless nights, hiding in caves and running for his life, before becoming the greatest king in the history of Israel.

God may choose to reveal to you the fullness of his plan and purpose for your life in the next five minutes, five years, or fifty years. But no matter how long the wait, choosing to wait faithfully will be much easier for you than choosing to wait miserably. But this is a difficult step to master. You have to focus on the reward that God says comes to those who choose to wait for him:

> Yet those who wait for the LORD
> Will gain new strength;
> They will mount up with wings like eagles,
> They will run and not get tired,
> They will walk and not become weary. (Isaiah 40:31, NASB)

If, like Heath, you find yourself frustrated over the uncertainty of your future, be encouraged. You're never alone. We'll have times when we're anxious to know where we're headed in life. And God understands how you feel. Rather than have you frustrated by the uncertainty, he wants you to use this time to rely on him even more. I know that waiting isn't on your list of favorite things to do, but learning patience is essential if you want to grow as a Christian. It could be that God has you right here in this moment because he too is waiting—waiting to have your undivided attention. Waiting patiently for you to give him all of yourself.

The waiting process may make you feel like a little kid lying in bed on Christmas Eve, anxiously anticipating the arrival of Santa Claus—and all the gifts he has for you. But really, waiting isn't a passive process. It requires action on your part. Which leads to the final question Heath asked in his letter.

Question 3: How Do I Live Out My Purpose?

First, be confident. Remember that one of the Foundational Truths of this book is: God's Word is truth. If he says it, he means it. Look at the promise God gives you in Philippians 1:6:

> Being confident of this, that he who began a good work in you will carry it on to completion until the day of Christ Jesus.

In his letter, it's obvious Heath is struggling with believing that God created him with a purpose. Heath assumed that because God had not fully disclosed this purpose to him yet, there was no purpose at all. You may be in Heath's position right now. It may not be time for God to fully reveal his plan to you. However, you can confidently move forward one day at a time, believing that God will finish what he started when he created you.

You may be thinking, *Jeffrey, how am I supposed to live out my faith confidently when I don't even really know what my purpose is?* Well, that's a great question. And fortunately I have a great answer for it.

Living out your purpose requires tremendous faith.

the Truth

Be firm in your faith. Stay brave and strong. (1 Corinthians 16:13, CEV)

Check out what Hebrews 11:1 says: "Faith makes us sure of what we hope for and gives us proof of what we cannot see" (CEV).

Even when you don't have all the answers, and even when the direction you should go in life is about as clear as mud, you've got to be willing to trust God if you want to find and live out his plan for your life. Even when it doesn't make sense. And even when it doesn't feel fair.

I know the word *faith* can be difficult to adequately define. For me, living a life of faith means that I strive every day to live more for God than I did the previous day. And tomorrow, I'll work to repeat that process.

The older I get, the more I realize that finding and living out God's plan for our lives isn't necessarily about arriving at a destination. Rather, it's more about a journey. With every step we should become more like him, and every day we should surrender more of ourselves to him. When we walk that path, our formation—our transformation—can continue.

I guess you could say then that the process of becoming the woman God made you to be doesn't end until you breathe your last breath. I think that's what Paul was describing in Ephesians 4:13 when he said, "This will continue until we are united by our faith and by our understanding of the Son of God. Then we will be mature, just as Christ is, and we will be completely like him" (CEV).

So, you've made me read almost this entire book just to tell me that becoming the woman God wants me to be is something that never ends. I'll never actually become that woman until I die? That's not what I wanted to hear. It almost sounds like things would be easier on my own.

Okay, I know at first it sounds pretty tough…and even disappointing. But really it's nice to know that, as long as you live, God's working in you to make you better. You never get to a point where God's like, "That's all I can do with you. This is as good as you'll get." There's always more good stuff to come. I know I'm still learning and growing in my relationship with God. I definitely don't have it all figured out yet. But I finally came to a point in my life where I was willing to completely surrender it all to him. I'm trying really hard to trust where he has me today and where he wants to take me tomorrow.

I guess...but that sounds kind of exhausting and scary.

Sure, it can be. But knowing I'm being made into something bigger than I'll ever become on my own helps me to remove the fear and just embrace the journey. Plus, God never makes mistakes, so what he's offering may sound hard, but the outcome will be better than anything you can do on your own.

Hear me clearly. It is *not* always easy to live the way I've described, especially when we live in a world that's trying to pull us away from God. So when you fail, don't beat yourself up. Just get back up and start again. Remember, being made into the woman he desires is not about perfection. It's about consistency.

My Space

What do you believe God is asking you to do with your life this year?

What one thing is God showing you that you need to do to grow in your relationship with him?

Write a prayer asking God to help you commit to this one thing.

Chapter 13

Fearless!

It's a scary place out there.
But *faith* is another word for "courage."

I love scary movies. Not the ones with blood, guts, and a psycho, but the ones with suspense, mystery, and a twist at the end that hits you upside the head out of nowhere. You know, like the last ten minutes of *The Village*. Or the final minutes in *The Sixth Sense*. And, of course, the full hour and a half of one of the greatest mystery movies of all time, *Scooby Doo*—the one where the mystery gang reunites on an island to investigate strange occurrences. Don't play dumb...you know you watched it.

Anyway, though you may not be a *Scooby Doo* fan, I bet you've seen a few movies that have left you freaked. But it's not just movies that scare us. Real life can be pretty frightening too. Choosing to live as a stander rather than a sitter will mean there'll be a lot of times when you're afraid—moments when it seems like you're the only one standing for what's right.

Obviously, God knew this would happen. That's why 2 Timothy 1:7 says, "God gave us a spirit not of fear but of power" (ESV).

However, sometimes it's hard to know that spirit is there. Look at what one teen wrote to me:

> Jeffrey,
>
> You spoke at my summer camp last year. I have never been challenged by anyone the way that you challenged all of us there. I am trying to apply the things to my life that you encouraged us to do. But the fact is it's difficult to live a life that honors God, especially at school. It seems like there aren't very many people in my school who say they are Christians. And even the few who say they are don't really live like it. I know that taking a stand for God is what's right, but sometimes it feels like I am the only one standing.

Sadly, this will be the case more times than you'd like. When I was younger, there were a lot of times when I felt like I was the only person in my school standing for what was right. Have you ever felt this way? I bet you have a time or two…or three hundred. And if you haven't yet, get ready, because living out God's purpose for your life will inevitably lead to some stand-alone moments.

It really stinks to feel like you're out there all by yourself on the right side of the fight. But you won't be the last to do it—and you definitely won't be the first. The Bible is chockfull of stories about fearless women who chose to stand for what was right. The lessons you can learn from them will help you live out God's purpose for you with courage and conviction.

Seize the Moment

In Exodus chapter 2, there is a Levite woman who gives birth to a son. Little did she know God would soon use this baby to help free the Israelites from 430 years of captivity. There have been countless books, sermons, and illustrations developed around the story of her son Moses. However, we hear very little about his sister, Miriam. Yet had it not been for her, Moses might have never seen his first birthday.

In Exodus 1:22, the stage is set for a story unlike any other in the Bible. The Egyptian Pharaoh gives "this order to all his people: 'Every boy that is born you must throw into the Nile, but let every girl live.' " Moses's mother puts him in a reed basket and sets him adrift in the Nile River. Watch what happens next:

> The baby's older sister stood off at a distance to see what would happen to him.
>
> About that time one of the king's daughters came down to take a bath in the river, while her servant women walked along the river bank. She saw the basket in the tall grass and sent one of the young women to pull it out of the water. When the king's daughter opened the basket, she saw the baby and felt sorry for him because he was crying. She said, "This must be one of the Hebrew babies."
>
> At once the baby's older sister came up and asked, "Do you want me to get a Hebrew woman to take care of the baby for you?"
>
> "Yes," the king's daughter answered.
>
> So the girl brought the baby's mother, and the king's daughter told her, "Take care of this child, and I will pay you."

> The baby's mother carried him home and took care of him. And when he was old enough, she took him to the king's daughter, who adopted him. She named him Moses because she said, "I pulled him out of the water." (Exodus 2:4–10, CEV)

Even though Miriam was young and probably really scared, not only for the safety of her brother but also for her own life (after all, she was spying on the royal family's daughter), she chose to set aside her fears and be a person of great courage. Not to mention she was really good at thinking on her feet. She quickly took the initiative to suggest, unbeknownst to Pharaoh's daughter, that the baby's mother take care of her own son. Brilliant! Moses's mother believed she would never see her son again, but Miriam wisely and bravely figured out a way to bring Moses back to her. Miriam waited for the right moment, and then seized the opportunity.

I wonder how many other girls would have responded as Miriam did. How much simpler and safer it would have been to *only* do what her mother asked, and no more. It would have been easy for Miriam to say, "I did my duty. I watched him and made sure he was okay," and then be done with it. Instead, she fearlessly approached Pharaoh's daughter. And the rest is history.

It's Not About the Spotlight

Moses grew up to be an incredible leader used by God to free his people from life under a brutal ruler. Through God, Moses performed many signs and wonders before Pharaoh that resulted in ten plagues. He eventually convinced Pharaoh to let God's people go. He led the exodus of over a million people out of Egypt. (I hope they packed a lot of toilet paper!) He marched them across the Red Sea on dry land. He brought the Ten Commandments to them and helped establish laws that we follow to this day. Moses led the Israelites for years through the wilderness before they finally reached the Promised Land. Yes, Moses was to Israel what Aretha Franklin is to soul, what Big Mac is to McDonald's, what...okay, you get it. He was an Israelite icon. But none of this would've happened had it not been for one very important behind-the-scenes person—Miriam.

Miriam played a critical role in preparing the way for God to use Moses to fulfill his plan. Miriam's choice to seize the moment and be fearless is a great story of a woman God used in an amazing way. And the coolest part of all is she didn't care if she was ever featured on the cover of *Israelite Illustrated.*

Our society values the winners, the stars, the ones who get all the attention, whether they really deserve it or not. But Miriam's story is proof that God isn't looking for the next supermodel, power broker, or rock star. He's just looking for a woman of character who is willing to be used, even if it means wading knee deep in the water and tall grass.

• • • • question

If God asked you to do something totally unglamorous and you knew you'd never get much credit for it, would you do it? If God called you to the darkest corner of the Amazon, would you go? If he summoned you to the desert of Najd, could you say yes? If God took you to the slums, the third world countries, and the poorest regions of the world, would you seize the moment?

It's Not About What Others Think

It was only a few days before Jesus would be arrested when he and the disciples came to eat with Lazarus and his sisters, Mary and Martha. Jesus had miraculously brought Lazarus back to life not long before. Mary had witnessed this incredible act, and she had great faith in him. This faith led her to do something surprising. Take a look:

> Six days before Passover, Jesus entered Bethany where Lazarus, so recently raised from the dead, was living. Lazarus and his sisters invited Jesus to dinner at their home. Martha served. Lazarus was one of those sitting at the table with them. Mary came in with a jar of very expensive aromatic oils, anointed and massaged Jesus' feet, and then wiped them with her hair. The fragrance of the oils filled the house.
>
> Judas Iscariot, one of his disciples, even then getting ready to betray him, said, "Why wasn't this oil sold and the money given to the poor? It would have easily brought three hundred silver pieces." He said this not because he cared two cents about the poor but because he was a thief. He was in charge of their common funds, but also embezzled them.
>
> Jesus said, "Let her alone. She's anticipating and honoring the day of my burial. You always have the poor with you. You don't always have me." (John 12:1–8, MSG)

These aromatic oils used by Mary to massage Jesus's feet were expensive ointments imported from the mountains of India. To put it mildly, this wasn't some off-brand lotion. This was expensive stuff, worth about a year's wage.

Mary gave up something that was worth a lot to her so that she could show her reverence for Jesus by massaging his feet with it. And then she wiped his feet—feet most likely weathered and dirty from walking in the heat of the day in sandals down a dusty road—with *her own hair*. What an incredible act of humility—and bravery.

Did you notice how immediately someone jumped in to criticize Mary for what she did? Surely she knew that what she was about to do would probably cause a stir among those watching. But did she care? No. She only cared about pleasing Jesus by doing what she felt led to do.

In a moment of fear, the lies are near:

- "Don't stand. You'll be the only one."
- "Go ahead, join in. It's just this one time."
- "If you don't join them, you'll be left out."
- "You don't really think you can stand up, do you? Don't do it—you'll lose."

And did you notice what Jesus said in Mary's defense? He said, "Let her alone. She's anticipating and honoring the day of my burial." Even though Jesus had tried to tell them many times, not even his disciples knew he was going to die in just a few days. Maybe Mary didn't know either. But she did what she was led to do, and she didn't ask for an explanation. She could have used those oils on Lazarus's body when he died. But somehow she knew to save them for Jesus. In her act of humility, she was making the statement that honoring the Savior of the world was even more important to her than honoring her own flesh and blood. Now that is a fearless woman.

Living as a woman in pursuit of God's will for your life can be a scary thing. Sometimes the circumstances of your life may seem unfair. And sometimes the things God asks you to do may not make sense at first. There'll be a lot of times when you're faced with questions that you just can't find the answers to.

But remember: Being fearless doesn't mean you'll have all the answers. It just means that you're willing to step out in the midst of questions because you trust that God has all the answers.

• • • give it a shot

The next time you feel like you're the only one willing to stand, remember that there could be many more sitting around, wanting to stand too, but they need someone else—you—to take the lead. Give it a shot and stand.

It could be there's someone in your life, maybe even a close family member or friend, who doesn't recognize you for the woman you're becoming. Maybe, like Judas, they can't understand what God is leading you to do. Don't let their lack of belief in you keep you from believing in yourself. Mary didn't let anyone shake her confidence. Living fearlessly is about having faith that God has your back.

This book has given you a list of qualities that define you as a woman. In moments of doubt and times of temptation, use that list to remind yourself of who you are. And then believe it.

• • • believe it

You are...

God's mirror
good
beautiful
a woman of commitment
a woman of purpose

the *Truth*

You are the ones chosen by God, chosen for the high calling of priestly work, chosen to be a holy people, God's instruments to do his work and speak out for him, to tell others of the night-and-day difference he made for you—from nothing to something, from rejected to accepted. (1 Peter 2:9–10, MSG)

This Is Me

Mary's act of humility and obedience was fearless. It's also the perfect story to end this book with, because Mary showed you that you should want to honor Jesus with your finest possessions, your money, your humility, your life...and even your hair. By doing what she did, Mary showed Jesus that she wanted to give him everything. And you should want to do the same.

Hold up. You almost had me. I was really starting to buy this stuff. But Mary was a good woman who did good things. I'm still not convinced I'm the kind of person who can do great things like that for Christ. I haven't always honored God with my life. Does he even want to use someone who's ignored his will so much?

Well, what if I introduced you to another Mary—Mary Magdalene. You've probably heard of her. She's the most famous of Jesus's female followers. And she was the first to see the risen Jesus and spread the news to the disciples. But before Mary Magdalene knew Jesus, she was far from perfect. Look at this:

> When Jesus rose early on the first day of the week, he appeared first to Mary Magdalene, out of whom he had driven seven demons. (Mark 16:9)

Wow. A woman once possessed by *seven demons* becomes the first to see the greatest miracle in all of history—Jesus risen from the dead. Mary Magdalene's past didn't matter to Jesus. He had driven the demons from her, and she became one of his most faithful followers. So he gave her the great privilege of heralding his resurrection.

There are countless stories of people in the Bible who didn't live spotless lives. But God chose to use them because, despite their mistakes, they still wanted to honor him. Living a fearless life for God doesn't mean you live a flawless one. God's not looking for perfection. Because it's impossible for you and me to be perfect. He just calls you to be the person he created you to be—a woman willing to live fearlessly for him. God's looking for a woman who'll simply say to him, "I want to give you more of me today than I did yesterday."

take a break

Are you a woman who's truly willing to let God use you just as you are?

If yes, write a prayer now and tell God exactly that.

If not, write a prayer to God and tell him how you feel. Share with him the things about yourself that are holding you back (maybe you don't feel smart enough, maybe you're too afraid of looking foolish, maybe you don't feel good enough). Be honest with him and ask him to help you overcome these fears so he can use you.

A fearless woman:

- chooses God's ways, even when they're not popular
- looks for a way out in a moment of temptation
- strives to please God in all things
- realizes her mistake, confesses it to God, and gets back on the horse and starts riding again

There'll be days when the world tries to convince you that you're not beautiful enough, smart enough, skinny enough, popular enough—just simply not "enough." Every day the doubters of the world will try to keep you from being the real you. Immorality will try to trip you up and make you feel unworthy. And there'll be Judas-like obstacles staring you in the face, telling you you're just being stupid and you'll never win.

Don't let any of it shake you. Just remember God created you *exactly* as he wanted you to be. And what he began in you, he will complete. All you have to do is stop doubting his plan and embrace the person he made you to be. Not the person the world thinks you should be. Not the person your insecurity makes you believe you are. But the person God saw before you were even born. That is who you are. And the more you work to be that person, the easier it will be to look in the mirror and say—proudly, *not* sarcastically—"This is *me*."